T0320060

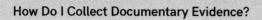

How Do I Collect Documentary Evidence?

ELGAR DISSERTATION COMPANIONS

Series Editors: Bill Lee, *Sheffield University Management School, The University of Sheffield, UK,* Mark Saunders, *Birmingham Business School, University of Birmingham, UK* and Vadake Narayanan, *LeBow College of Business, Drexel University, USA*

Elgar Dissertation Companions will be valued by postgraduate students embarking on their dissertation as part of their taught Masters programme. Providing more content and direction than general research methods texts, these books will save the reader time and energy to confidently produce the best dissertation they can.

Each book will provide all the knowledge that a Masters student requires to use the method or methodological approach when designing research or collecting and analysing data in preparation of their dissertation. The series will evolve to incorporate new and innovative methods not currently available as and when the methods have reached a level of maturity to be taught in Masters programmes.

Although the books are targeted at students reading for a Masters degree, they may also serve as reference books for doctoral students and faculty members.

How Do I Collect Documentary Evidence?

BILL LEE

Professor of Accounting, Management School, The University of Sheffield, UK

Elgar Dissertation Companions

Cheltenham, UK • Northampton, MA, USA

Published by
Edward Elgar Publishing Limited
The Lypiatts
15 Lansdown Road
Cheltenham
Glos GL50 2JA
UK

Edward Elgar Publishing, Inc.
William Pratt House
9 Dewey Court
Northampton
Massachusetts 01060
USA

A catalogue record for this book
is available from the British Library

Library of Congress Control Number: 2021936621

This book is available electronically in the **Elgar**online
Business subject collection
http://dx.doi.org/10.4337/9781839104725

ISBN 978 1 83910 471 8 (cased)
ISBN 978 1 83910 473 2 (paperback)
ISBN 978 1 83910 472 5 (eBook)

Printed and bound in Great Britain by
TJ Books Limited, Padstow, Cornwall

Contents

List of figures and tables   vi
List of illustrative boxes of fictional students' research   vii
Glossary   viii

1   Introduction   1

2   Philosophical underpinnings   12

3   Components of text in documents   27

4   Collection and compilation of text in documentary
     research   47

5   Examples of published studies using documentary
     evidence   76

6   Conclusion   81

Bibliography   91
Appendix: sources of documents   96
Index   100

Figures and tables

FIGURE

2.1   Domains of reality   16

TABLES

2.1   Positions arising from permutations of ontological
        and epistemological ideas   14
2.2   Relationship between philosophical position and
        type of logic   17
2.3   Relationship between philosophical position, type
        of logic and purpose of collection of documentary
        evidence   19
3.1   Impact of research strategy on decisions of what
        documents to collect and how to organize their collection   29
4.1   Example of a spreadsheet for recording information   55
4.2   Documentation of development of research ideas
        and strategy   58
6.1   Summary of approaches to studies based on the
        collection of documents   82

Illustrative boxes of fictional students' research

2.1	Nnamdi's survey 1	20
2.2	Simone's interpretative study 1	21
2.3	Ahmed's critical narrative study 1	23
2.4	Miao's study of the constitutive quality of documents 1	24
3.1	Nnamdi's survey 2	34
3.2	Simone's interpretative study 2	38
3.3	Ahmed's critical narrative study 2	41
3.4	Miao's study of the constitutive quality of documents 2	45
4.1	Nnamdi's survey 3	49
4.2	Nnamdi's survey 4	51
4.3	Nnamdi's survey 5	53
4.4	Simone's interpretative study 3	59
4.5	Simone's interpretative study 4	61
4.6	Ahmed's critical narrative study 3	66
4.7	Ahmed's critical narrative study 4	68
4.8	Miao's study of the constitutive quality of documents 3	70
4.9	Miao's study of the constitutive quality of documents 4	74

Glossary

Abduction – A form of logic that may start with an empirical observation but which will move iteratively between the available evidence and theory to develop the best possible explanation that is available in the current circumstances.

Actants – A physical or digital form that may play an active role in interaction with humankind.

Analysis – Entails breaking a phenomenon manifest in evidence into relevant components to produce data in the form of patterns in the evidence.

Case study – The study of an event, phenomenon, organization, individual as worthy of research in its own right, rather than because it has been drawn from a wider population. It is often suggested that a case study occurs when the focus of the study cannot be separated easily from its wider context and the conduct of the study will entail collection of several types of evidence.

Comparative case study – The study of two or more events, phenomena, organizations or individuals that have some similarities and differences and which are worthy of study in their own right, but which, by comparison, provide opportunities for theorization around the reasons for their differences.

Constructivism – A theory of ontology that views people bringing their own unique understanding to social situations which, thus, help to shape the world of which they are a part.

Critical realism – A philosophical position that affords recognition to causes of events in a real world, but which may not be observable by humans who have the capacity to develop forms of understanding, some of which will be erroneous.

Data – Evidence that has been subject to processing to provide an interpreted reading or understanding.

Deduction – A form of logic which uses theoretical propositions that are believed to be true, to infer further propositions or hypotheses that may be tested through the gathering of empirical evidence.

Discourse – Language as a collection of symbols that are used to convey meanings within a specific institutional, historical and social context.

Document – A repository for conveying symbols for utilization of interpreted meanings across time and space.

Documentary artefact – The medium on which a record may be stored, such as paper or film.

Epistemology – Theory or understanding of the nature of knowledge.

Event – An outcome of human activity, often conceived in advance.

Evidence – Information that may be used to help substantiate an academic explanation.

Generalization – Inference that an explanation or theory that is applied to one set of circumstances may also apply to other sets of similar circumstances.

Induction – A form of logic that uses empirical observations to formulate theories and explanations.

Interpretative realism – A philosophical position which accepts the existence of an external reality that should be interpreted through the perspective of the humans experiencing an event or phenomenon.

Interpretive / interpretivism – A range of theories of epistemology in the social and management disciplines which acknowledge that humans have the capacity to interpret the circumstances that they encounter and make a choice of different responses.

Logical-positivism – A philosophical position that seeks to apply logical propositions to the objective understanding of an external reality evident in the epistemology of positivism and the ontology of realism.

Monophonic – An academic account that gives precedence to one voice.

Narrative (critical) – An account about an event, phenomenon or process that is likely to have the characteristics of a story, including a plot (and possibly sub-plots) that starts with a beginning and proceeds through a chronology to an end, in which characters play an important role. The characters may have the roles of heroes, heroines, saviours, villains, etc., which are provided by a frame of reference that seeks to promote affinity with particular characters in the plot of the story and its outcome. A critical narrative will be written from the standpoint of somebody other than the most powerful participant who is likely to have provided the formal account of the phenomenon.

Ontology – Theory or understanding of the nature of existence and being.

Particularization – A theory that confines its explanation to a specific event or set of circumstances.

Polyphonic – An academic account that expresses differences between a range of voices.

Positivism – A theory of epistemology based on observation of the world as an external reality, objectively free from value judgements.

Realism – A theory of ontology based on an understanding of a reality existing externally to – and independently of – human consciousness.

Research strategy – The organization of underlying philosophical assumptions, research objectives and means of enquiry into a plan of action. The research strategy may be emergent, as the plan of action is changed as obstacles are encountered.

Sampling (random) – The selection of units to study from a wider population. A simple random sample aims to select units that are representative of that wider population because each unit has been given an equal chance of inclusion in the sample.

Survey – A study where the purpose for the information gathered is aggre-gation to understand a population, or similarities and differences between sectors of that population.

Symbolic interactionism – A theoretical approach which views the different signals that individuals emit and their interpretation by others with whom they are interacting as central to the understanding of social phenomena.

Temporal brackets – Organization of time into a chronological sequence according to the importance of the events in that sequence rather than according to simple chronometric measurement.

1   Introduction

The objectives of this chapter are to:

- define a document;
- explain the origin of the use of documents in business and management research;
- discuss a range of sources of documents for use in business and management research and outline a range of approaches that should inform how documents are collected;
- introduce four fictional students undertaking their Masters-level dissertation whose research projects will be used to illustrate the steps reported in subsequent chapters;
- outline the rest of the book.

Introduction

Documents are an essential and ubiquitous part of organizational life and play an important part in management. Documents may define what members of an organization see as its essence, such as in mission statements, or they may report on its constitution and composition, such as in agreements around mergers and lines of authority. Documents may provide formal records interpreting what occurred at the organization in the past, such as with minutes of meetings and annual reports and financial records, or they may provide prescriptions of what the organization would like to happen in the future, through policy statements and strategic plans. Documents may be used in the conduct of a range of different functions across an organization such as providing details of a company's income and expenditure in accounts, promotion of its brands through its marketing materials, details of ordering of operations and production schedules for different manufacturing or service departments, reports on its governance arrangements, and policies explaining how its human resource department may handle disciplinary or promotion cases. These are just some examples of formal documentation.

There are many other ad hoc materials, ranging from those that have some formal sanction such as emails, notes and notices, to more informal materials including regurgitation of stories and accounts of organizational folklore, jokes and details of social arrangements sent between colleagues that provide insights into the culture of an organization. There are also a wide range of external documentary sources such as consultant reports, trade magazine and business press commentaries, customers and former employees reviews, noticeboards, pressure groups' publications and international, national and local government documents that provide insights into others' perceptions of the management of organizations. All of these materials, if collected and organized systematically, could provide details of how an organization is managing its operations, or how successful the organization is, or what its members, customers and others think about its management; in other words, provide answers to a wide range of research questions and hypotheses. Yet documents are perceived by some (e.g., Ahmed, 2010) to be a marginalized method of research. One reason for this may be that while there are a number of academic sources on how to analyse documents when undertaking research (e.g., Bowen, 2009; Hodder, 2003; Lincoln, 1980; Pryor, 2008a), there are fewer sources in the business and management field on how to collect them systematically to facilitate conduct of analysis.

This book helps to fill that void by introducing different research strategies related to different philosophical positions to guide the systematic collection of a range of different research hypotheses or questions. Four particular research strategies will be used in the course of this book, namely: a survey, comparative cases, composition of a critical narrative and identification of constitutive texts. Acquisition of the knowledge about the collection of documents will also help when writing the methodological section or chapter in your project report or dissertation so that you can explain your research strategy in a systematic and detailed way that elaborates on the assumptions that you have made and the procedures that you have adopted to collect and order the materials. Such a systematic and detailed account will enable the reader to understand the value of the research that you have conducted. Documents may be divided into those which may be considered as providing secondary evidence because they are produced for a purpose other than the research and often predate its conduct, and documents that are deemed to provide primary evidence because they have been created specifically for the research. This book focuses principally on the former, that is, collection of documents that are created independently of the research.

Documents may be given different degrees of importance in a research strategy. For example, they may provide only part of the evidence in a study that draws on other sources such as interviews and observations. Or they may be the sole form of evidence that is used. This book assumes that you will only collect documents in your research, although the same approaches to collecting documents may be adopted when you are intending to supplement documents with evidence gathered through other means. It should be stated clearly at this stage that if you are conducting a study where you rely wholly on documents, it is important that you recognize the limits to what you will be able to report before starting to collect documentary evidence. All that you can portray is what the document – or the author of the document - is representing, rather than what actually happened if the document claims to be the record of an event, or what the author would like to happen if the document is stating a policy rather than what will actually happen. If you formulate research questions that are seeking more than this, you should use another method for collecting evidence either instead of or as a supplement to the collection of documents.

Having intimated at the ubiquity and usefulness of documents, the remainder of this chapter will first define what constitutes a document and what this implies for the process of collecting documents. It will then describe the origin of documents as a source of evidence in management research, before outlining how the rest of the book will unfold to help collect documents systematically in a variety of ways according to your philosophical predilections, to help in the conduct of your research. Finally, four hypothetical students will be introduced who intend to use documents in their research, but who will encounter some of the decisions that you may face in your research, to illustrate how you might overcome such challenges.

Defining documents

The multifaceted qualities of documents have led different authors to offer different definitions of documents. For example, Hodder (2003, p. 703) has described a document as 'mute evidence ... [which] unlike the spoken word, endures physically and thus can be separated across space and time from its author, producer and user'. Hodder's definition is useful because it expresses the way in which documents allow information to be transposed both temporally and spatially. However, not all documentary records are 'mute'. Over the past couple of centuries, an increasing variety of forms of records have emerged that are able to project sound and/or vision as well as the written word. These include film, digital versatile discs, compact discs and pages in cyberspace. Many are not mute in the sense of emitting no sound, although they may be unheard and unseen unless the researcher includes their manifest qualities in the research design. Hodder's definition also implies a degree of universality in the meanings that may be represented by any symbols that are contained within a document. We will see in Chapter 2 that while some philosophical positions do suggest that there is such a correspondence between the written word and a single reality, others challenge whether this is the case.

Not surprisingly, the potential for such objectivity is challenged by others' definitions of documents. Pryor (2003, p. 2) has argued that documents may have 'creators (agents, writers, publishers, publicists and so on), users (readers, or receivers) and settings'. The settings provide an institutional context that could affect the way in which information is received and interpreted. Pryor (ibid.) thus argues that all 'three realms are implicated in the emergence of documentation'. Pryor's definition has the strength of introducing the idea that an author's intended meaning when creating a document has the potential to vary from the understanding that users derive from the document, which could be influenced by the regulatory and institutional setting including language, belief systems and legal requirements. Pryor (2008a, 2008b) subsequently highlights how documents may serve as actants – that is, hybrids of objects and actors. Thus, Pryor (2008b, p. 824) says, 'documents serve not merely as containers of content, but as active agents in episodes of interaction and schemes of social organization'. When this potential is recognized, documents may be seen as having relational properties with other actors, helping to structure relationships both between the documents and the actors and between different actors in the environment in which the documents are employed. For example, in the human resource field, a document may state the way in which those holding superordinate positions in a hierarchy should conduct appraisals of applications that others put forward for promotion. The relational and potentially political dimensions of documents have explicit recognition in the definition of documents provided elsewhere. In effect, Lee (2012a, p. 391) defines a document as:

> a durable repository for textual, visual and audio representations that may be retained and used in different times and spaces, creating the possibility that the meanings of the representations may be interpreted differently – and employed accordingly – by the user, partly because of variations between the regulatory and institutional setting of the producer and user of the document. The user may either be the researcher or another actor in a setting where the documents are employed and the employment of those documents may – or may not – advantage some parties or disadvantage others.

It is this definition that is assumed in the rest of this book. The focus of the book is, however, on the written textual dimensions of documents which tends to be central to most research involving documents (Tight, 2019, p. 9).

Although this book is not about documentary analysis, it is necessary while they are being collected to have some understanding of how documents will be used subsequently, if the most appropriate documents are to be collected. As Walliman (2011, p. 2) reminds us, collection of evidence is not separated neatly from analysis in a qualitative research project, but 'analysis is often carried out concurrently with data collection'. So it will be necessary in this book to take occasional excursions into the realm of analysis to help identify what documents are required and what characteristics need to be present in the documents to justify their collection. The first excursion takes place here, when we consider what constitutes analysis.

Everyday definitions present analysis as a detailed or systematic inspection of the contents or components of the topic of focus. Academic definitions extend analysis beyond what it entails, to also include its purpose. For example, Blaxter et al. (1996, p. 185) write that analysis entails 'the search for explanation and understanding in the course of which concepts and theories are likely to be advanced, considered and developed'. It follows from this that documentary analysis involves the systematic organization and inspection of documents as a durable repository providing representations for the purpose of developing ideas and advancing theories. The written textual contents of documents may be collected for a range of reasons such as comparison or aggregation with the contents of similar documents, interpretation of the intended meanings of authors, sequential records of the unfolding of a series of events, or indications of how someone is seeking to persuade others of the authenticity of a path of action. Having defined documents and the qualities that help in deciding which ones to collect, it is appropriate to ask whether there is a history of documents being perceived as a credible form of evidence in business and management research.

Origins of documentary research in business and management research

Documentary artefacts providing signifiers of meaning are probably as old as humankind. Hieroglyphic representations on cave walls or on pottery and biblical references to Moses' tablets of stone indicate early existence of the use of symbols and codes to record messages. There are many sources that attribute the invention of paper and its manufacture – a prerequisite for the easier production of documents – to China around 100 BC and AD 105, respectively. Collection of documents for research purposes probably came much later, as Krippendorff (2019, p. 10) attributes the inception of documentary analysis as a systematic interrogation of written text to 'the inquisitional pursuits by the Church in the 17th Century'. Although there is extensive evidence of accounting records being kept many centuries ago to record income and expenditure of tradespeople, the modern genesis of much documentation relating to management and businesses suitable for research purposes can probably be attributed to the development of factories in the United Kingdom (UK) in the eighteenth century and the subsequent Joint Stock Companies Act of 1844 which facilitated the establishment of large businesses as separate legal entities utilizing the assets of several individual, detached owners. This created a requirement for the routine sharing of information between people who may have been dispersed geographically. There is certainly evidence that both Marx in his analysis of the creation of value in capitalist economies in his opus *Das Kapital*, and his collaborator Friedrich Engels in his *The Making of the English Working Class*, drew on formal documents such as Factory Acts that sought to regulate workplaces to inform their theorizations. A number of authors (Braverman, 1974; Rose, 1978) have attributed origins of modern management thought to the scientific managers who had a presence in the United States of America (USA) and a number of European countries including the UK, France and Germany at the beginning of the twentieth century. Brown (2005) reports that pioneers of 'Scientific Management' such as Gilbreth (1911) prepared documents proposing reconfigured bodily movements for industrial workers to realize efficiency as parts of time and motion studies.

The generation of businesses and management documentation is one phenomenon, but in order for such documents to be used in research there also needs to be the development of academic faculty that recognize the useful contribution of those documents to help explain why business and management phenomena are as they are. There are indicators that researchers had developed the tools for utilizing documentary evidence in other social sciences by the 1970s (Krippendorff, 2019, p. xiii). However, such developments probably took place later in the business and management fields. In many countries, business and management schools developed after other social science disciplines. The USA has dominated the academic study of management for the past century (Honig and Bedi, 2012). The prominent position of American business schools was assisted when the influential Ford Foundation report, authored by Gordon and Howell in 1959, prompted massive funding to improve research training (Mangematin and Baden-Fuller, 2008, p. 214; see also, Cooke and Alcadipani, 2015, pp. 485–486). Ford Foundation funding also helped in the export of American ideas of management and business schools to a number of countries, including India (Kothiyal et al., 2018; Mir et al., 2004; Srinivas, 2008), other parts of Asia, Africa and Australasia (Qi, 2012), different European countries including France, Italy, Spain and Turkey (Kipping et al., 2004; Üsdiken, 2004), Israel (Frenkel and Shenhav, 2003) and Brazil (Cooke and Alcadipani, 2015). Development of business and management schools and related research took place in a number of other countries subsequently. For example, in the UK, many business and management schools were not established until after the expansion of higher education following the 1963 Robbins Report, and in some instances – such as the different entities named Judge at the University of Cambridge from 1990 – much later. Notably, the first journal of the British Academy of Management, the *British Journal of Management*, was inaugurated in 1990.

Since the establishment of business and management faculty with an interest in conducting research, there have been a number of factors that have both facilitated – and been symptomatic of – the collection of documents for research purposes. Firstly, there has been the advent of the internet and the related digitalization of catalogues of both contemporary and historical documents, making it increasingly easy for researchers to collect such materials for their studies. Secondly, there has been the fusion of disciplinary ideas most prominently evident in areas that combine history with business subjects such as accounting history and business history. Relatedly, academies have developed their own special interest groups of academics focused on historical dimensions of disciplines. For example, the British Academy of Management's (BAM) Management and Business History special interest group was formed in 2015 and the British Accounting and Finance Association's Accounting History special interest group was formed in 2018. Concern with history often involves researching documentary sources, and communities of academics interested in the fields of accounting history and business history provide the opportunity for meeting and exchanging experiences from collecting evidence. The special interest groups interested in accounting and business history have joined longer-standing collectives interested in the development of research methods, such as the American Academy of Management research division which was formed in 1988, the Research Methodology special interest group of BAM which was launched in 2005, and the Research Methods and Research Practice strategic interest group of the European Academy of Management (EURAM) which emerged from 2008. The interest of these groups includes the collection of both historical and contemporary documents for research purposes. The work of the scholars who form these groups and have utilized documents in their research has been showcased in articles in a range of business history, general management and research methods journals, helping to advance understanding of how to collect useful documents. Such articles have informed the preparation of this book.

Sources of documents for research purposes and a range of strategies

As indicated in the introduction, there are a wide range of different sources of documents that are useful for business and management research, in addition to those produced by an organization. When research is being conducted into an organization, or an event associated with an organization, it is also useful to look at the organization's own issuance of news stories. Increasingly, organizations have archives of their own news stories on their websites. Addresses of other sources where you may find useful documents are shown in the Appendix, but it is of value to introduce genres of documents very briefly to indicate some of the things that you might find from them. Newspaper reports are useful for learning about both the phenomenon which you wish to study and its sequence. They are also useful for gathering evidence of contemporaneous and contextual events to those that are studied. Trade and consultancy reports are valuable for the provision of accounts of particular organizations. Professional associations' documents are useful for understanding the expectations that bodies may have of some organizational members. There are a wide range of official sources, including those providing government abstracts of sectors, accounts of government expenditure on particular departments and projects, reports of debates and enquiries in parliament, and list of publications on a broad range of issues. There are a range of bodies that provide details of the functioning of markets. There are also review websites that provide the opinions of consumers of services.

When seeking out sources of documents, it is important to be purposive in your approach and to think of why those documents are being collected. A range of strategies may be adopted for the collection of documents. A particular type of document from a whole population of organizations – such as corporate social responsibility reports of the Financial Times Stock Exchange (FTSE) top 100 companies, the FTSE 100 – could be collected if one wanted to conduct a cross-sectional survey of a particular type of organization for some reason. Different types of documents about a single organization – such as its own documents about its work processes, newspaper reports, commentaries by former employees from review websites – could be collected if the objective was to compile a case study or a number of case studies for comparison. A historical trawl could be performed to collect a chronology of reports of a sequence of events to provide a narrative around a theme from a particular voice, either as a commentator, or through empathizing with a participant, as every narrative should have a narrator's voice (Pentland, 1999). Alternatively, documents may be collected both of an author involved in a particular event and from a broader context with the intention of finding out how an author has influenced that event. Each of these different strategies will be elaborated as the book proceeds.

An introduction to four fictional students about to embark on a Masters-level dissertation

Four fictional students undertaking their Masters-level dissertation will be used to illustrate the thoughts, considerations and actions that might affect the adoption of one or another of the research strategies identified above, and approaches to the collection of documents outlined in the remainder of this book. The four students are as follows. Nnamdi is a Nigerian student studying for a MSc in Accounting and Finance and is going to conduct a survey based on documents. Simone is a French student who is studying for a MSc in Leisure Management and will collect documents to compare cases. Ahmed is a UK student studying for a MSc in Human Resource Management and will compose a critical narrative using documents. Miao is a Chinese student studying for a MSc in Marketing and is seeking to examine the constitutive qualities of documents. They share a flat with each other. In the subsequent chapters we will see how they design research and collect documents differently for their respective dissertations.

Outline of remainder of book

It is now appropriate to outline the remainder of this book and what to expect from each chapter. Chapter 2 introduces different ontological and epistemological approaches and the way in which permutations of different ontological and epistemological position could inform different types of study based on documentary research. Chapter 3 explains the components of different types of approach to the collection of documents. Chapter 4 explains how to operationalize the different components to collect documents in a systematic way to generate useful evidence in a research project. Chapter 5 provides published examples of different studies that relied on documentary evidence. Chapter 6 discusses the strengths and weaknesses of relying on documents in research. The types of strategy in the collection of documentary evidence that are listed in

Chapter 2 are cross-sectional surveys of a population of a similar type of document performing the same explicit purpose, collection of documents providing interpretation of experiences of the same general set of facilities, collection of a chronologically sequenced set of documents that express a narrative of an event, and collection of documents that indicate how their users are constructing means of reality for others to adopt. These distinctions are followed through in the subsequent chapters, so Chapter 3 reports on the components of each of the respective approaches, Chapter 4 shows how to operationalize the respective approaches, Chapter 5 reports published studies that use those approaches, and Chapter 6 reports both generic strengths and weaknesses of documentary analysis and strengths and weaknesses of the different approaches. As, in each chapter, the different approaches appear in a separate section, it is possible to go through the book reading only the sections that relate to your chosen approach. However, you are advised, strongly, to read through the whole book to start with, as this will help you to understand how the approach that you adopt differs from other approaches. Only then is it sensible to flip between the pages that focus on your approach.

Summary

This chapter has defined documents. It has provided an account of how documentary research has gained legitimacy in the business and management field, identified different sources and strategies for collecting documents in a research project, and introduced four fictional students who will each pursue one of those strategies when collecting documents for research. Finally, it has provided guidance on how to read the rest of this book.

2 Philosophical underpinnings

The objectives of this chapter are to:

- introduce different ontological and epistemological traditions that inform business and management research;
- outline ways of theorizing with documentary evidence depending on the approach adopted when collecting evidence;
- link the different ontological and epistemological traditions and ways of theorizing to types of approach and strategy adopted for collecting documentary evidence.

Introduction

Any academic research project – including dissertations – will have underlying philosophical assumptions. The rigour of academic work appears enhanced when these assumptions are acknowledged at the outset of a project, built into the design of the research to guide the collection of evidence and written up subsequently when the research is presented. Two sets of assumptions that are of importance here relate to views about ontology and epistemology. Ontology is important because it relates to what our understanding of existence is, so it will affect what we see as constituting a document and what capability we may perceive in a document. Epistemology is important because it will affect our view of the value of the representations that are contained within a document. This chapter has three substantive sections that each have a distinctive purpose. The first provides a brief overview of some of the ontological and epistemological positions that inform management research. The second links these different positions to different ways of theorizing from documentary evidence. The third then connects both the chosen epistemological and ontological position and the approach to theorizing, to different plans for action when collecting documents.

Philosophical assumptions

The potential uses that a researcher will see for a document will depend in part on the researcher's philosophical leanings. It has been suggested elsewhere (Lee and Saunders, 2017) that the spectrum of ontological positions may be simplified to form an axis along the range from realism, where people view a reality existing independently of the researcher's – and others' – perception, through to extreme forms of constructivism where reality is deemed to exist only in the minds of the participants. In between these polar points, there are perspectives that recognize different dimensions of reality which, although constructed through interactions of different people or actors, have varying degrees of endurance and permanence (see, e.g., Llewellyn, 2007). Epistemological assumptions may also range along an axis from positivism that assumes that it is possible to analyse the social world, using a scientific method to separate out the researcher's values and view an objective truth which positivists perceive as the purpose of research, through different positions that acknowledge a possibility of producing a shared, consensual understanding within a specified social milieu, to interpretive positions that perceive each actor as having their own distinct understanding and so the purpose of research is the capture of those shared meanings or individual interpretations. Some writers view the two axes reported above as running parallel with each other, so that a realist ontology is equated with a positivist epistemology to offer an objectivist position, and a constructivist ontology is equated with an interpretive epistemology to provide a subjectivist position. While some overlap between different types of epistemological and ontological position is acknowledged, acceptance of total congruence is not the position adopted here. Instead, a fourfold classification that offers a different combination of the two axes, as used previously by Lee and Saunders (2017), is used here. The different combinations of ontology and epistemology are shown in Table 2.1.

To explain the contents of the table, logical-positivism appears in the top left quadrant. Logical-positivists view reality as existing independently of observers. An objective, observational language parallels that reality, which allows understanding of that reality by reading what is said, written or represented in a document. So, as long as the text of a document is grammatically correct so as to remove any ambiguity, and visual images are accurate representations, the same single message will be understood by anyone perusing a document. That shared single understanding may then be used to advance a collective understanding through the development of logical propositions and hypotheses to test against evidence, including that manifest in documents. Moving downwards to the bottom left corner, there is an incongruity – which produces an incoherent logic – between a constructivist ontology that views reality as a product of specific individuals' interactions, and a positivist epistemology that views a reality as independent of particular individuals. Moving to the upper right quadrant in the table, where a realist ontology is combined with an interpretive epistemology, such theorists will recognize that there will be some parts of organizational life that have an existence independent of the participants – such as the building in which their work-life takes place, or the paper or computer on which messages are recorded and stored – even if their understanding and interpretation of such records are not predefined by either the building or the means of storing the records. Interpretive approaches – such as phenomenology – are concerned with ways in which people experience their world in the specific contexts that they occupy. Social meanings are at the centre of any analysis. Thus, documents contain signs and symbols that have to be interpreted. Moreover, the way in which the signs and symbols are formatted will be subjected to conventions that prevail in a particular culture. Any interpretation of what those signs are intended to symbolize, or how they are received, must be linked to the culture in which the author prepares the document and the reader digests its contents. The important objective is to capture the meaning of the interpretations of the participants.

Table 2.1   Positions arising from permutations of ontological and epistemological ideas

Ontology ↓ Epistemology →	Positivism	Interpretative
Realism	e.g., Logical-positivism	e.g., Critical realism, Interpretative realism
Constructivism	Incoherence	e.g., Symbolic interactionism

Two combinations of an interpretive epistemology with an ontology of realism will be considered here. The first is interpretive realism. Interpretative realism has been defined in various ways, depending in part on the disciplinary background of the author. A general social science definition is provided by Denzin (2009, p. 100), who reports that interpretative realism entails researchers inserting 'their personal interpretations into the life situations of the individuals studied'. This definition will be adopted here. So words in a document provide the means for the researcher to read and impute meaning to the intent of the author of the document about the situation that is being described. The second combination of an interpretative epistemology with an ontology of realism considered here is that of critical realism. Critical realism has been espoused by many authors, but it is perhaps most often associated with the late Roy Bhaskar (1975, 1978, 1989, 1998). Like other realist perspectives, critical realism accepts that the world may exist independently of how we perceive it. Bhaskar (1998) argues that there are two forms of knowledge: the transitive and intransitive objects of knowledge. Intransitive objects of knowledge have causes that exist independently of how humans perceive them. By contrast, transitive phenomena are systems for interpretation of events, that are generated by humans. The different types of knowledge mean that the observer is fallible and the knowledge generated may not be accurate.

Linked to the objects of knowledge are Bhaskar's (1975) concepts of different domains of reality. These may be represented as in Figure 2.1. Firstly – and consistent with intransitive objects of knowledge – there is the real domain which provide underlying structures and processes that may manifest in events and phenomena in the actual domain. While these manifestations in the actual domain may give some indication of the real domain, not all of the real domain will necessarily be observable and so sense may be made of the actual domain using transformative objects of knowledge. Yet we may not observe all of the actual domain and the empirical domain comprises that which is observed. It follows from this that information represented in documents provide some record of a phenomenon that has taken place in the actual domain, even if the phenomenon is simply the production of the record. The documents provide a means for researchers to produce an instance of a transitive phenomenon in the form of an explanation or an account or narrative of an event, even if the underlying structures in the real domain that caused the events are not seen or understood by anyone.

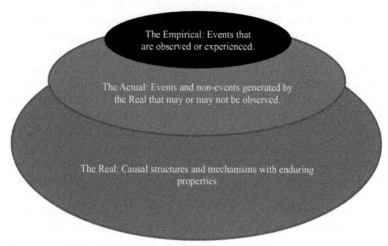

Source: Developed from Bhaskar (1975, 1978).

Figure 2.1   Domains of reality

The final position that is considered here is that of symbolic interactionism. Symbolic interactionism has been associated historically with
the work of Herbert Blumer (1969). The term 'symbolic interactionism'
provides an exemplary explanatory title for the combination of the interpretative epistemology and the constructionist ontology, which views
people attributing symbols and understanding to things such as physical
entities, relationships and abstractions such as ideas, interpreting the
symbols offered, and deciding how to interact with others in the construction of reality. This is not to argue against the existence of patterns
in social interaction as, over time, people's interactions serve to generate
shared meanings which lead them to have shared expectations in their
interactions. Codes as manifest in words and pictures are, thus, symbols.
A corollary of this perspective is that language, images and other contents
of documents are important symbols that people either have used or are
using in their construction of reality. In this regard, symbolic interactionism may be seen as a precursor of what Rorty (1979) has described as the
'linguistic turn', where language is seen as constructing reality rather than
reflecting it.

To summarize the usefulness of documents in research from the different
philosophical positions outlined above, logical-positivists would view

documents as containing language, pictures, and so on, that correspond with an external reality, and so documents may in themselves be seen as objective representations and their collection would facilitate understanding that external reality. Both interpretative and critical realists accept that there is an external reality, but documents may provide only a partial and not necessarily accurate representation of that reality, although they can provide insights into how the authors of those documents understood that reality. Symbolic interactionists will see documents providing a basis for symbols that people have used in the construction of reality. It is now appropriate to consider how the collection of documents might facilitate theorization in research, as this have an impact on the choice of documents to collect.

Approaches to theorizing

There are three broad types of logic for theory-building: induction, deduction and abduction. It is possible to apply any of the three to the different epistemological and ontological perspectives for understanding documents that have been identified thus far, although some are either more suited to, or have been historically associated with, particular types of philosophical positions, as summarized in Table 2.2.

Table 2.2   Relationship between philosophical position and type of logic

Philosophical position	Logical-positivism	Interpretative or critical realism	Symbolic interactionism
Type of logic	Deductive	Abductive	Inductive

The correspondence between an external independent reality and an objective language means that there is a tendency to believe in the cumulative nature of scientific knowledge, which suggests a deductive logic. Deductive logic involves using existing propositions on premises which one believes to be true and proven, to infer another proposition or hypothesis, to test by the gathering of empirical evidence using a scientific method. Hence logical-positivism promotes a belief that it is possible to derive propositions from existing scientific knowledge reported in academic articles, to put forward a hypothesis about something that we have not yet had confirmed. An example may be the following: (1) documentary evidence shows that firms in the motor car industry with clearly stated whistleblowing policies reported on their websites perform better financially than firms in the motor car industry that do not have such policies; (2) documentary evidence shows that some companies in the building construction sector are now stating their whistleblowing policies on their websites while others are not doing so; therefore, (3) we can hypothesize that firms in the building construction sector that are stating their whistleblowing policies on their websites will outperform those that are not doing so. It is then possible to collect documentary evidence of any whistleblowing policies and of the financial performance of the building construction firms to establish whether this proposition holds.

Different types of logic may be employed with interpretative and critical realist positions, but arguably these philosophical positions fit most neatly with abductive reasoning. Abductive reasoning may entail observing a particular document as an empirical instance, then 'selecting or inventing a provisional hypothesis [or theoretical proposition, that is] … better than any other candidate hypotheses, and pursuing this hypothesis through further investigation' (Kennedy and Thornberg, 2018, p. 53). In the context of this book, that would be collecting further relevant documents to understand whether they facilitate further theoretical development. As Kennedy and Thornberg (ibid.) have stated:

> In abduction, qualitative researchers use a selective and creative process to examine how the data support existing theories or hypotheses as well as how the data may call for modifications in existing understandings. They go beyond the data and pre-existing theoretical knowledge by modifying, elaborating upon, or rejecting theory if needed, or putting old ideas together in new ways to examine, understand, and explain the data.

In this way, the observation of people's experiences and views expressed in documents provide the empirical instances that may be examined iteratively with theories about the external world to generate the best possible explanation.

Finally, induction may be seen to offer the best fit with symbolic interactionism. Inductive logic entails generating theoretical ideas based on the prior observation of instances of social activity to identify the pattern that arises. Thus, symbolic interactionism that views people constructing their world through their interactions – albeit ones that give rise to patterns due to expectations based on prior assumption – infers that understanding may be obtained through inductive logic. So it may be that it is perceived that the issuance of one type of document by an organization, such as an application for planning permission to expand a factory close to a green-field site, is followed by other documents such as other submissions by opponents to the application and protest letters to a newspaper. We may then observe whether such documents as applications for planning permission elsewhere prompt documents containing similar or different types of responses, and theorize from those observations.

Having suggested links between types of logic and different philosophical positions, we now turn to appropriate ways of organizing the collection of documents when adopting a particular philosophical position and type of logic.

Approaches and strategies for the collection of documentary evidence

Four types of approach or evidence collection strategy will be articulated to inform the ways in which documentary evidence is to be collected. The four approaches are: surveys, comparative cases, a critical narrative and a deconstruction of the text. These different approaches will be linked here, respectively with logical positivism, interpretative realism, critical realism and symbolic interactionism and the types of logic shown in Table

Table 2.3   Relationship between philosophical position, type of logic and purpose of collection of documentary evidence

Philosophical position	Logical-positivism	Interpretative realism	Critical realism	Symbolic interactionism
Type of logic	Deductive	Abductive	Abductive	Inductive
Purpose for collecting documents	Survey	Comparative cases	Critical narrative	Identification of constitutive texts
Student	Nnamdi	Simone	Ahmed	Miao

2.2, to provide the summary in Table 2.3. We will explore these different approaches through the respective examples of the hypothetical students who were introduced in Chapter 1.

A logical-positivist position, that views text in a document as accurately representing an external reality, permits a researcher to believe that – as long as the documents are available – it is possible to survey a population of a genre of documents to perceive the patterns found in the document as reflective of the reality at the organizations that produced the documents. This is illustrated by the example of Nnamdi in Box 2.1.

Box 2.1 Nnamdi's survey 1

Nnamdi had been encouraged by the lecturers on his Masters in Accounting and Finance course to read financial articles in the press in order to stay abreast of relevant financial issues. He had just read an article which reported that, for various reasons, the previous year had been a very poor year for growth in the United Kingdom (UK), with the economy only growing by 1 per cent. That gave him an idea for his dissertation, which he was thankful for, as he had a meeting tomorrow with his dissertation supervisor, Professor Mark Right. Nnamdi knew that some of his lecturers questioned whether corporations' financial statements were accurate – although Mark Right was not one of them – but he reasoned that because of regulation and auditors' examination and verification of the accuracy of those accounts, they could be assumed to be as true a representation as anything could possibly be. He thought that what he could do was obtain the financial statements of different companies, look at their overall financial performance and profit before tax last year and compare it with the performance and profit before tax of the preceding year, to see whether it was less than, or matched or exceeded the 1 per cent growth that was reported to have existed across the economy as a whole. Nnamdi thought that he could employ the following deductive logic:

Proposition 1: Good companies outperform the economy.

Proposition 2: The economy grew by 1 per cent.

Proposition 3: Therefore, companies that had growth greater than 1 per cent were good companies.

Nnamdi thought that he could also read through the financial report to look for any factors indicating why some organizations grew by more than 1 per cent to help explain what is a good company. He hoped that Mark Right would like his idea.

Nnamdi's story continues in Box 3.1 in Chapter 3.

Interpretative realism accepts that there may be an external reality, but that people may perceive that reality differently. While what is written and how it is written in a document may be culturally specific; documents on the same topic will enable researchers to attain some appreciation of how the authors of those documents are viewing that reality, even if it is acknowledged that the researcher may be using their own interpretation of the meanings of others when looking at the documents, which shared cultural understanding will enable. This is illustrated by the example of Simone in Box 2.2.

Box 2.2   Simone's interpretative study 1

One day, Simone decided to take a break from reading for her tutorial on epistemological positions for the research methods module on her MSc in Leisure Management. She decided to go into the lounge where Nnamdi was already relaxing. They got talking and Nnamdi asked Simone what she did over the summer and whether she had managed to take a holiday.

Simone answered that she had gone on holiday with friends to a holiday resort. Nnamdi asked Simone whether she had enjoyed the holiday, and Simone answered that she had thought she would, as she and her friends had agreed the resort together, they had all detailed the facilities that they wanted and the resort that they had chosen met all of their needs in terms of facilities, so they all thought that it would be perfect. However, when they arrived, they experienced the resort differently. The friends of Simone who simply went to clubs at night, got up and laid by the pool reading books all day, really enjoyed the time. Simone enjoyed it less. She liked going to clubs, but did not want to stay out as late as her friends, and was often disturbed by noise when others were returning to their rooms. Simone was also a competitive swim-mer and participated regularly in swimming galas and competitions. When she was at home, Simone would go to her local pool four times a week. The local pool had 'lane swimming' which allowed her to swim up and down in lanes at speed to maintain her competition-ready fit-ness. However, she had found that the pool at the holiday resort was always too full of other holiday-makers to enable her to swim at speed unobstructed. Reflecting on her philosophical assumptions, Nnamdi asked rhetorically: 'Isn't it funny how people can experience the same place so differently?'

Nnamdi's question prompted Simone to think about her preparations for the tutorial that she had been preparing for. She responded, 'You know, I have just been thinking about this, as in the research methods lecture last week the lecturer was talking about how people might be realists and accept that there is an external reality, but that we might all experience and interpret the same reality differently.' In that mo-ment, Simone decided on a general research question of what influenc-es people's interpretations of their experience of holidays when staying at hotels and guest houses in the UK at different points of the year. She thought that her philosophical standpoint would combine a realist ontological position with an interpretive epistemology. She also real-ized that she was embarking on a form of abductive logic, as she had started with an empirical observation of her own experience, but could now move backwards and forward between empirical observations and literature as she sought the best possible understanding of what influ-ences people's interpretations of their holiday experiences.

Simone's story continues in Box 3.2 in Chapter 3.

Critical realism also accepts that there is an external reality, although – as we have seen above – people may not necessarily be able to view that reality, but will only see manifestations of that reality in the actual world. Documents' representations of that world provide empirical insights which may provide their authors' narrative of events, but their contents may also be combined to provide an alternative narrative that the researcher constructs. This is illustrated by the case of Ahmed which is reported in Box 2.3.

Box 2.3   Ahmed's critical narrative study 1

Ahmed had chosen to do his MSc in Human Resource Management because for one of his summer holidays during his undergraduate studies, he worked in the head offices of a multinational corporation. During the time he worked there, his department moved offices. In the early part of his employment, the department was based in an old building where the company had been situated for the past 65 years. In the latter part of that summer, the department was based in a new modern facility. Moving offices was a complete relief, as that summer was really hot and the new offices had a modern thermostatically, controlled ventilation system, which allowed Ahmed and his colleagues to remain cool on even the hottest days. In the early part of the summer, in the old office, conditions were often unbearable as there was no air conditioning, and even opening the windows had little effect on days when there was no breeze. On one day, conditions were so hot that one of his colleagues fainted, and the whole department stopped work in protest against the conditions. They were only persuaded to go back to work for the remaining two weeks in the old building when senior management agreed for the doors to the office to be kept open, with large, mobile industrial fans situated just outside to blow air into the office, and for each person to be provided with a smaller electric fan on their respective desk. Senior management also agreed that cold drinks would be distributed to them hourly, and new cool water dispensers would be situated in the office.

One day, early in his second term, Ahmed was in the library preparing for a tutorial on industrial conflict, and one of the tasks that he had to conduct was to research the causes of a recent industrial dispute. He was quite excited to find details of a current strike by employees at the warehouses of an online retailer, because of working conditions. The action was particularly interesting to Ahmed because when he was looking for jobs for the preceding summer, before he found the position in the office discussed above, he had considered applying to this organization. It had run television advertisements in his region about how good it was to work there, and reported on the benefits that employees had. Now, there was a strike. Ahmed decided that when he had to write his dissertation next term, he would study the causes of that strike.

As he left the library he met Nnamdi, who had also been in the library researching for a tutorial on philosophical perspectives for his research methodology course. Ahmed asked Nnamdi what he had been reading. Nnamdi told Ahmed that he had been reading an article by Sue Llewellyn (2007) on critical realism, and explained that critical realists believed that there is an external reality, but people may not necessarily see all that reality and are capable of generating different explanations of the parts of the reality that they do see. Nnamdi said that Llewellyn's paper was interesting because she identified different dimensions of a situation that were more durable than others, and so would be less susceptible to change in the short term. Ahmed recognized immediately the value in Llewellyn's arguments as he thought back to his employment over the summer, and how senior managers had failed to perceive how hot the original office was and the effect that it had on people. He also remembered how it was possible to introduce ad hoc changes to ventilation in an office in the short term, and a much better ventilated situation through the construction of an office block over the longer term. Ahmed decided that he would adopt a critical realist position for his study of the dispute at the online retailer. Although he did not realize it at the time, Ahmed was also embarking on an application of abductive logic, as he was starting with some empirical observations of the organization where the dispute was taking place, and was going to move between theories in academic literature and other documentary evidence as he sought an explanation for the dispute.

Ahmed's story continues in Box 3.3 in Chapter 3.

Symbolic interactionism views the contents of documents as important symbols that authors use or are using in their construction of reality, which will then influence how others may interact both with the documents' authors and with others affected by the documents. This is illustrated by the case of Miao that is shown in Box 2.4.

Box 2.4   Miao's study of the constitutive quality of documents 1

As Ahmed, Nnamdi and Simone argued about at which restaurant they should start their weekly night out together, Miao reflected upon the questions of: if she was a product to be marketed by the university, what type of product would she be, and how was she being constituted by the education that she was undertaking as part of her MSc in Marketing, and how was she contributing to the education that her peers was receiving, and to how her lecturers saw their experience as educators? This train of thought led her to think more deeply about the different lecturing styles of her lecturers when they delivered the material on their modules. She noticed that they had completely different styles when sharing information. The lecturer Tony Jones, who taught the 'Marketers' Toolbox' module, emphasized legal and regulatory requirements. Miao thought that Tony's slides were prescriptive in stating that the procedures outlined in the course had to be applied earnestly to ensure that marketers engaged in honest and truthful campaigns. Tony's slides thus often contained clear regulatory statements and instructions of exactly how to organize marketing campaigns. By contrast, the 'International Marketing' lecturer, Karen Gooding, often reported on concepts such as 'glocalization' and 'international diversity management', and her slides would define concepts of fast food restaurants and state how such definitions of rapid processing of standard dishes had global and universal meanings, but how experience of such concepts were not the same because corporations such as McDonald's adjusted their menus to suit tastes that were 'local' to particular countries, and so people would experience fast food differently in different countries. Miao thought that Karen's slides were trying to persuade students to perceive fast food as a real entity, even if it was experienced and interpreted in different ways in different countries. Miao wondered whether Karen's slides were not representing concepts such as glocalization as real entities to persuade students of their usefulness and, thus, constructing knowledge in a particular way. Miao then thought about the lecturer Alison Owen, who led the 'Green Marketing' module. Alison seemed to spend a lot of time in the lectures asking questions about who marketing was for, and the consequences of tourists 'invading' areas labelled as 'beauty spots', disturbing local residents and wildlife and leaving litter behind, while polluting the air and exhausting finite resources by burning fossil fuels in their cars. Her slides often included pictures such as extinct dinosaurs, and questions of what should and should not be marketed. Alison did not provide answers to the questions, and Miao's peers walked out in a state of confusion, but in Miao's current reflections she saw it simply as another form of discourse used in the construction of knowledge, albeit one that was more open-ended than the others.

Miao thought that it seemed as though Tony was constructing knowledge from a positivist standpoint, Karen was constructing knowledge from an interpretive position, and Alison was constructing knowledge from a constructivist position. Miao wondered whether she could write her dissertation on how marketing knowledge was constructed by lecturers according to different underlying philosophical perspectives, and she thought about whether her lecturers would allow her to use material from their respective modules to do that. Miao also recognized that she would be employing an inductive form of reasoning, as she would be basing her explanation of construction of knowledge in lectures on empirical observations of documents in the form of her lecturers' slides. Just then, she heard Simone say, 'So we are agreed that we will start at the Taj Mahal restaurant on Essex Street', so Miao went off to get ready to go out.

Miao's story continues in Box 3.4 in Chapter 3.

Summary

Having reported on epistemological positions, ways to develop theory and related strategies to inform the collection of documentary evidence, the next chapter turns to the issue of preparing for the collection of documents.

3 Components of text in documents

The objectives of this chapter are to:

- show you how to prepare for a study based on documentary evidence;
- show how choice of different type of approach will structure the relationship between review of the literature and start of collection of evidence;
- introduce a range of concepts that are relevant to the different approaches of surveys, comparative case studies, critical narratives and constructivist studies when collecting documents.

Introduction

Studies based on the collection of documents are considerably varied. This makes it impossible to provide absolute guidelines on how to collect the documents, as this will depend on a variety of factors, including your epistemological and ontological assumptions, as discussed in Chapter 2. Nevertheless, to complete your project successfully, it is important that you adopt a systematic procedure which includes:

1. Defining how each document that is collected is related to your research questions or hypotheses. In other words, what exactly is the value of the representation in the document to be collected?
2. Justification that the documents that are collected have a relationship to other documents that may be part of the same study, but are distinct from all other documents that are not being considered in a particular project.

3. Application of a logical process to select the documents that you collect from all others to realize your overall purpose.
4. Collection of those texts in a systematic way to ensure the potential for the identification of patterns and meanings that – after analysis – you can write up in the context of the relevant literature to complete your research project.

The last point will be addressed in Chapter 4. The first three points are considered in this chapter. Table 3.1 provides a summary of the types of decisions that might be taken to address the first three points above when pursuing each of the four different approaches or document collection strategies – of surveys, comparative case studies, critical narratives and constructivist discourses – that were identified in Chapter 2. As the research strategy helps to shape the collection of the documents, the remainder of the chapter will elaborate in turn on how a researcher, who pursues each of the four strategies, addresses the four questions in the table. In doing so, a number of assumptions are made. Firstly, that the researcher is concerned primarily with contemporary documents. This tends to be the case with management students – with the possible exception of those interested in business and management history – who seek to interpret and understand contemporary phenomena through current academic literature. Thus, it is simply noted here that if one is using historical documents, it may be necessary to conduct a number of checks to ensure that the documents are authentic. The second assumption that is made is – because of the short time that Masters students have available – the documents will be collected via the internet rather than by visiting archives. If archives are to be visited, then more time needs to be available and the researcher needs to familiarize themself with the protocols of the archives to be visited, including their opening times, what materials the researcher may take into an archive's reading rooms, how many documents may be ordered at one time and how long it takes the archive's staff to retrieve the documents.

Before turning to consider how researchers may pursue each of the strategies and address the issues in Table 3.1, it is of value to make comments about two general important considerations when planning to collect documentary evidence. The first is how to identify documents. Important tools to help in the collection of documents from the internet are search engines. There are a considerable number of these available, the most popular of which include Ask, Bing and Google. Although there will

Table 3.1   Impact of research strategy on decisions of what documents to collect and how to organize their collection

Strategy → Decision ↓	Survey	Comparative cases	Critical narrative	Discourse
What does each document represent?	Units of occurrences	Phenomena, events and organizations, or different accounts of those phenomena, events and organizations	Incidents affecting relevant parties	Representations of beliefs
How to perceive and justify?	Representatives of population	Type(s)	Sequential moments	Potential influences of behaviour
How to select?	Blanket or random sampling?	Theoretical selection	Occurs within temporal bracket(s)	Theme relating to behaviour of interest
Why/ objective/ ultimate purpose	Generalization, or reasons why certain units vary from generalization	Particularization	Moral story	Event origin/ history

be some overlap, each search engine is likely to lead you to a different set of webpages, even when using the same search terms derived from your research questions or hypotheses. Thus, to ensure the most comprehensive coverage for your particular topic, it is sensible to use more than one search engine. It is important, however, when conducting the search, to note the search engine(s) and search terms that you used in each search, and on which days you conducted the search. This will form part of the audit trail that you will create – along with recording details of the sites from where you retrieved particular documents that you use, and when – to report in your methodology chapter to demonstrate to the reader that you have been systematic in the collection of the evidence in your dissertation. The second general consideration relates to ethical issues. Universities have ethical procedures that anyone conducting research has to observe, and it is important to find out what is permitted by your own institution's guidelines and regulations when planning your research. Each research project generates its own ethical quandaries. It is tempting to assume that when we retrieve documents that are already in the public domain, there has already been the resolution of ethical issues that arise with other research approaches such as informed consent and the right of research participants to withdraw from the research. Such assumptions are based on an insensitive – if not erroneous – belief that a document that is in the public domain is a public resource. With any document, there is always the danger that reproducing parts of it without permission could infringe copyright. Another important consideration is whether the author of the document really intended to surrender all proprietary rights when putting the document in the public domain, and whether, if the author knew the purpose to which a document was going to be used, they would have presented the information in the way that it is presented. Without recognition of the proprietary rights of the author, the researcher assumes not only shared ownership of the document once it is in the public domain, but also shared ownership of the meanings conveyed in the document. Thus, it is important to consider whether the same sensitivity may be shown when collecting documentary evidence as would be shown when collecting other forms of evidence.

Some documents, such as companies' and other organizations' annual reports and their webpages, have been prepared for public consumption and so this issue is less of a concern. This is also the case with statutes and other documents placed in the public domain by governmental authorities. Other forms of documents – such as autobiographies – are published and sold commercially when some proprietary rights are transferred to the purchaser as long as no laws are broken in exercising the limited proprietary right. Once the documents are collected, some forms of analysis will involve aggregation and so the researcher will only be reporting on patterns which again limit any violation of individual authors' rights. The advance of social media does provide many new opportunities to gather information about different organizations' activities and many people's opinions, beliefs, and so on, that they have not provided for research purposes. Kozinets (2019) has suggested that there is a consent gap between public perceptions of how social media may be used and requirements under the General Data Protection Regulations. If there are particular documents produced by a small number of individuals that are important to your research, and the identity of the authors are known, it is appropriate to request permission to use the documents in the way that you intend. If the authors are not known and the documentary evidence has been gathered from a particular social network, it may be appropriate to report your intended use to the administrators of those websites and ask whether they have objections to such use. Regardless of whether it is possible to obtain these types of consent, unless it is essential to report on the identity of individuals, such as in proven fraudulent behaviour that led to the collapse of a company that may be being studied as part of a dissertation on corporate goverance, it is important to seek to ensure the same degree of anonymity as would be offered when collecting evidence through other methods such as interviews. This may require limiting direct reproduction of material as evidence when writing up your research (Tischer, 2020).

The chapter will now turn to considering how researchers may pursue each of the strategies – and address the different issues – identified in Table 3.1.

Conducting a survey of documents

What does each document represent?

As indicated in Chapter 2, researchers conducting a survey are most likely to draw on a positivist epistemology and realist ontology that will perceive the text, images, figures and numerals that appear in a document as mirroring and providing a representation of phenomena that exist in the external world. A document is thus a particular unit of record of that world. In considering the issue raised above of defining research questions or hypotheses that are to be answered with documentary evidence, it is important that those research questions or hypotheses embrace the unit recorded in the document. For example, under condition A, unit B is likely to react through behaviour C. From the context of marketing, we might say that eye-catching media advertisements for summer clothes in good weather lead companies using those advertisements to sell more summer clothes than clothes manufacturers who do not have such advertisements. In the context of human resource management, we might say that when corporations keep employees informed of all aspects of their business through newsletters, those employees are less likely to leave and those corporations will have lower labour turnover than organizations that do not use newsletters for this purpose. The consequences of both greater or lesser sales and more or less labour turnover might be checked by reference to other documents.

How to perceive and justify

How the document is to be perceived will depend in part on the research questions that are being asked or the hypotheses that are being proposed, and whether those questions and hypotheses are addressed to the phenomenon that the document is recording, or to the documents themselves. Either way, it is possible to perceive the document as either a unit or a representation of a unit in a wider population. To illustrate the distinction that is being made here, corporations registered on stock markets are obliged to produce annual reports. Some may choose to include in those reports tables of philanthropic work that they have conducted. We could see those tables as accurate representations of reality and ask how many organizations are engaged in philanthropic initiatives and what form does the philanthropic initiative take, or we could ask the question of the reports in terms of how many reports contain details of philanthropic acts. What it is important to emphasize here is that the unit belongs to – and may be seen as representative of – a wider population. To address the issue of justifying the collection of the documents, it is necessary to be able to present them as belonging to that wider population. Being clear on the contours of the population will set the boundaries to the search for documents, as the documents of primary interest will be those that pertain to the population. For example, the population could be cafes, clubs of a particular type, restaurants, organizations or corporations of a particular size or in a particular location. It is important to be confident in setting those parameters that all units in that population have been included.

Sometimes there are readily available lists of organizations whose documents might be collected, such as the top 100 companies in the Financial Times Stock Exchange (FTSE), the FTSE 100, or firms of accountants affiliated to the Institute of Chartered Accountants in England and Wales (ICAEW) or some other professional body, or local councils listed with the Local Government Association. There are other populations for which there might not be lists available, such as restaurants in a town. It may be possible to use a proxy that provides a partial list, such as a telephone directory that has a list of restaurants that advertised themselves as such when the telephone directory was compiled. This may require some checking to see the extent of its continued usefulness. Whatever method is adopted for defining the limits to the population, it is important that this is recorded before the start of the collection of documents, and that any additions and the reasons for those additions are recorded when they take place during the documentation collection process. This information will then be included in the discussion on the methodology of the project. It is at the stage of defining the population to be studied that it is also important to consider whether the documents are going to be readily available in sufficient abundance to address your research questions or hypotheses.

There are some types of documents that we know will be readily available for collection because there are legal obligations for them to be produced. For example, publicly listed companies are required to produce annual statements of their financial accounts, and there is always a narrative that accompanies these accounts. There are others that we may also be able to acquire by visiting the organization's website. For example, restaurants are likely to have their menus readily available. With other documents, such as a human resource policy, it is less likely that the documents will be in the public domain and it may be necessary to email, write to or phone the organization in order to acquire the documents. While this is feasible with a project where one has more time, such as a PhD, it may not be possible in the time permitted for a Masters-level project. So the recommendation here is to conduct a check on the internet by using a search engine to establish whether the documents are freely available. If the materials are not available immediately by looking on the websites of your population of organizations, and if it is not easy to identify sources through such a trawl, consider a different project or set of research hypotheses.

How to select the documents

In many ways, it is important to understand the population when conducting any type of survey, including a survey of documents. As it is the level of the population that is likely to be addressed in research hypotheses – which provides the rationale for conducting a survey – the selection of the documents should be done in a systematic way that will allow inferences that the documents collected are representative of the wider population. The systematic way of collecting those documents will start with defining the method for the selection. Depending on how the unit has been defined in the research question, it may be possible to collect documents from the entire population, or what may be described as a blanket survey. For example, if the units to be studied are population of the FTSE 100 corporations in order to address a research hypothesis, it would be possible to collect documents from all of the organizations through their websites. Such a hypothesis may be that FTSE 100 corporations that have a major part of their business in the extractive industries are more likely to use their website to report on issues relating to their response to climate change than FTSE 100 corporations that do not have a major part of their business in the extractive industries. If, however, we wished to ask the same question across all companies that have limited liability, we would first need to identify all companies that are registered. In the United Kingdom (UK), it is possible to do this through Companies House. Then, the companies whose documents were to be studied could be selected randomly using a probability sampling technique that gave each of them an equal opportunity to be studied, or a degree of stratification which would select companies randomly within defined groups such as the stock market on which they were listed – for example, the Main Market and the Alternative Investment Market of the London Stock Exchange – to ensure that corporations of different, specific sizes are included. As will be seen in Chapter 4, the collection of texts in a systematic way will also involve preparing a sheet that allows recording of the information that is required from each document collected. The recording sheet would include the important independent, dependent and moderating variables that appear in the research hypotheses.

Ultimate purpose

Related to the focus on the population, the purpose of surveys of documents – like other surveys – is to establish patterns of nomothetic qualities in social phenomena. The product of this is either generalizations, or reasons why certain units within populations vary from a generalization. Let us return to the case of Nnamdi, in Box 3.1, who wants to study units of corporations in the entire population of the FTSE 100 to establish the extent to which the performance of the FTSE 100 was consistent with the performance of the economy as a whole.

Box 3.1   Nnamdi's survey 2

Nnamdi went to Professor Right's office for his first dissertation meeting. Professor Right asked Nnamdi whether he had an idea of what to research as a dissertation topic, and Nnamdi explained his idea about investigating the performance of the FTSE 100 corporations vis-à-vis the general small increase in growth in the economy as a whole. Mark Right said that he thought it was a very good topic, and it was good that Nnamdi already had a clear idea of a standard against which he could measure the performance of individual firms. Professor Right asked what factors Nnamdi thought would be important in influencing the performance of an organization. Nnamdi said that he was not sure, but he intended to look at corporations' annual reports to see what factors they mentioned. Professor Right said that he believed that Nnamdi should look at the academic literature in advance of looking at corporations' annual reports, to see what the literature had to say about the topic so that Nnamdi could frame original hypotheses that addressed the existing literature. Professor Right provided Nnamdi with a list of readings on the impact of chief executive officers' and other directors' performance and how a corporation's adoption of a policy of corporate social responsibility affected its financial performance.

Professor Right said that Nnamdi had a good idea, but he had a lot of work to do before the next meeting. He said that he wanted Nnamdi to go away and review the literature and come back with clearly stated hypotheses, framed by the literature but addressed to outcomes not already covered by that literature, a definition of the population and justification for selecting that population, details of the sources of information that Nnamdi would collect to test the hypotheses and a tool for recording the information that he collected. Professor Right said that Nnamdi would need some time to read the literature and so he suggested that they meet again in four weeks. Before Nnamdi left, Professor Right also recommended that Nnamdi looked at some of the literature on attribution theory, as some authors had argued that directors of corporations will report in annual reports that they were responsible for good performance and the broader conditions were the reason for any dimensions of poor performance, and he recommended that Nnamdi give some thought to this. Professor Right also recommended that if Nnamdi had some idea of how he was going to collect information before their meeting, he should make his application for ethical approval, stating that his suggested approach was still subject to approval by his dissertation supervisor.

Nnamdi's story continues in Box 4.1 in Chapter 4.

The study of comparative cases

What does each document represent?

Chapter 2 outlined how comparative cases complement a realist ontology where cases may exist in an external world, but an interpretive epistemology because people may encounter different instances of the same broad phenomenon and different understandings of why such a phenomenon has occurred. The documents will thus be perceived as providing representations of different instances of the same genre, or different interpretations of the same instance. When defining research questions to study via comparative case studies, it is important that the research question embraces the idea of comparison. So, for example, if it is different accounts of the same phenomenon, the phenomenon is likely to appear in the research question. In the area of employment relations, it might be asked how different perceptions of management and employees contribute to an industrial action. Documents produced by management and employees as well as those produced by third party commentators could help to compose different accounts of the same event. Alternatively, where the cases are of different events, the research question will focus on the differences that are important, and documents would be gathered about each of the events, with attention in the documents being focused on understanding the explanations of the reasons for the differences in the events.

How to perceive and justify

The composition of comparative cases when using documents will entail either different accounts locked together around the same event, or different instances of the same type. How those accounts are perceived will depend in part on the research questions that are being asked. The research questions are likely to provide an indication of the basis for comparison. They will state the type of organization, phenomena, events or processes in which the researcher is interested. The documents will thus be collected and justified according to whether they provide insights into the types of phenomena, and so on, in which the researcher is interested. It will be important to consider whether the documents are going to be readily available in sufficient abundance to address the research questions. This may require some revision of the research questions. It is probably not sensible to formulate research questions rigidly when looking for available evidence. A more sensible approach is to move between the initial research questions and the available evidence, modifying the former as knowledge of the latter is developed.

How to select the documents

As indicated, the research questions will guide the researcher towards the type of documents to be collected. In addition to selecting cases where there are sufficient documents, it is also important to consider the theories that are being used and the way that the cases may be used to address the theory, and the logic that will be employed. Following the arguments in Chapter 2, and the acknowledgement above that it is not necessarily possible to decide on the exact form of the research question until it is confirmed that there are sufficient documents, comparative case studies may complement the abductive logic, with an initial theory being chosen to suggest cases at the start, and then the theory is modified, or an alternative is chosen because it is better suited to elaborate on cases where there is evidence available.

Ultimate purpose

Comparative cases are useful for examining existing theories, but there is also another important reason for deploying case studies. As Lee and Saunders (2017) report, case studies may be used for the purpose of particularization of explaining why a particular case is as it is. In this regard, the comparative nature of the cases may both facilitate drawing the boundaries to the application of a theory, and explain the particular reasons why another genre of the same type is different. As will be elaborated in Chapter 4, in order to do this it is necessary to develop a tool to record information from the documents as they are collected, so that it is possible to make comparisons and identify differences, and to identify gaps in evidence and what more information needs to be collected as the research progresses. Thus, it is important that the tool for recording information about each case has identical headings – that relate to the components in the research questions – to facilitate that comparison. For illustration of the discussion so far, let us return to the story of Simone in Box 4.2, who wants to study different people's accounts of their experiences at cases of types of hotel, to establish the particular reasons behind the same facilities being experienced differently.

Box 3.2   Simone's interpretative study 2

Simone went to see her dissertation supervisor, Dr Tina Rowlands, to agree on her topic and her general research question of what influences people's experience of their holidays when staying at hotels and guest-houses in the UK at different points of the year. Tina asked Simone whether the types and level of facilities influence people's experience, and whether it would be sensible to simply survey the types of facilities that each hotel offered. Simone conveyed the details of her holiday experience from the previous year that she had told to Nnamdi (see Box 2.2 in Chapter 2) and explained that she thought that the same facilities could be experienced differently by different people.

Tina asked some more questions, including whether the hotel experience might also be affected by the weather at the time of the holiday, because in times of good weather, people might want to be outside the hotel while in bad weather they might also want to be inside. Simone agreed. Tina asked Simone how she was going to know whether people had been on holiday and would have something to report about their experiences. Simone said that she would ask them to think back to their most recent holiday. Tina said that was unlikely to work for comparative purposes, because people would not have been on holiday at the same time, and some people might have ideas that are fresh in their memories while others might not. Tina asked Simone how she would know whether the people had been to the same hotels, to have experiences of the same facilities. Simone did not have an answer, apart from surveying all hotels, which Tina suggested might take too long. Simone was beginning to think that her research question for her dissertation was wholly impractical, when Tina asked whether Simone would mind if Tina made a suggestion. Simone was pleased about this intervention. Tina said she always reviews the places where she stays on *Tripadvisor*, and asked Simone whether it would be a good idea to identify the same number of hotels in different types of location – namely coast, country or city – and list their facilities by visiting the websites of those hotels, and then look at *Tripadvisor* for reviews of the people who had visited those hotels over a specified number of months to see how they interpreted their experiences in their reviews according to: (1) the weather; and (2) the unit of the visitor, such as a lone traveller, part of a couple, a family with young children. Simone thought that this would be a good idea.

Tina concluded their meeting by asking Simone that before their next meeting in the following week, she: (1) came up with refined questions; (2) identified the documentary sources from which she could collect the above information; and (3) prepared a tool for recording the information that was collected and necessary to answer the refined research questions, in ways that would make the analysis easier.

The story of Simone's study continues in Box 4.4 in Chapter 4.

Critical narrative

What does each document represent?

Like comparative case studies, critical narratives complement a realist ontology where phenomena exist in an external world, but an interpretive epistemology is adopted as people may perceive different parts of the same phenomenon which lead them to have a different vision of the phenomenon, or they may interpret the same parts of the phenomenon in different ways because of their different life experiences, values, and so on. In this context, documents may be seen as representing a record, reflecting the values of the commentator, of one or more incidents in the particular event or phenomenon in which the researcher is interested. The phenomenon to be analysed could be a simple, single event such as a meeting to make a decision about a budget for a particular year. Alternatively, it could be a longer sequence of events, such as a period of industrial action, the implementation of a marketing strategy, the consequences of the adoption of a particular human resource policy, or the general performance of an organization across a year which followed an event such as the setting of too tight a budget, a damning newspaper report or a reduction in a rating provided by a credit rating agency. The documents that are collected will thus represent different accounts of the same phenomenon, or they will permit the composition of knowledge for interpretation of different instances of the same phenomenon. When defining research questions to study for a critical narrative, it is important to define both the phenomenon and the party whose viewpoint is to be adopted. For example, if it is the detrimental consequences of installing a large hypermarket on the outskirts of a village, the phenomenon may be the detrimental consequences of the placement of the hypermarket, and the viewpoint will be that of the villagers.

How to perceive and justify

The incidents that are recorded in documents will be perceived in a critical narrative as incidents in a sequence that will provide the events around which the plot or story of the narrative will take place. As there will be a plot to the narrative, when collecting documents it is important to always be sensitive both to the overarching event or phenomenon of interest and to how the details in one record may be linked to others. The criterion for deciding which documents to collect – and hence the justification for their collection – is that they contribute to an understanding of the story, and this criterion should be explained when you come to write up the details of your methodology. Of course, some events are considerably newsworthy and there appear to be an infinite number of documents about them. There are different ways of addressing such a problem of overabundance of evidence. One important way is by refining the research question – and hence the criteria for collecting the documents for the narrative – by limiting the time period that will be covered, or the particular parties involved in the events that will be given attention in the narrative, or the media outlets which will be used to provide information in the narrative. Such modifications should feature clearly in the refined research questions and be explained in your explanation of your methodology for your research. Of course, the opposite situation of too few available documents may also exist. If, when collecting documents, there appear to be too few sources and the information contained within each appears not to link readily with others, it is wise to revisit the issue of whether there are sufficient documents to study the phenomenon, or whether the research question needs to be revised.

How to select the documents

When deciding on which documents to collect, it is important to keep in mind that with a narrative there will be a start point and an end point to the story. Setting both the start point and the end point will help in the selection of the documents. It may also be sensible to break down the sequence of events into temporal categories, both to order the collection of documents and to check that documents are being collected about all of the important points. This does not have to be organized into a simple day-by-day chronology. Langley (1999) describes a tool of temporal bracketing. The idea of temporal bracketing allows the organization of material into broad, potentially uneven, brackets. For example, if one was interested in the impact that a legal ruling on representation in advertising had on the way in which specific products were marketed by an organization, three broad categories would be: firstly, marketing before the ruling; secondly, the process of the legal ruling including legal arguments being put; and thirdly, marketing after the ruling. As indicated above, additional criteria for selection of documents from others could be the individuals whose activities in events they report, or the media source that is reporting on the sequence of events which are essential to the narrative.

Ultimate purpose

The ultimate purpose of this type of approach is to provide a narrative. The narrative will need to have a beginning, middle and end, through which there will be a clear order or sequence of the events that take place. There will also be a plot or story which will highlight the significance of particular events in that sequence. The narrative will also have focal actors (Pentland, 1999). These may have particular characteristics that are common in stories, such as heroes, villains, victims, and so on. The characteristics of the focal actors will be defined largely by their relationship to the events that take place in the course of the narrative. Information about the plot of the story and the characters will need to be kept in mind as the information is collected, and the way in which this may be done is elaborated in Chapter 4. There will also be a commentator on the events that are taking place to provide the narrative. This is likely to be the researcher, although the researcher could adopt the perspective of one or more of the focal actors and explain the events from their perspective. Most significantly, the narrative will be an expression of values, and so it will have an evaluative frame of reference through which the key events in the sequence will be interpreted. The narrative will also provide other contextual information that will provide signals to the reader of how the different events are to be interpreted. Let us return to the story of Ahmed in Box 3.3, who wants to study the events relating to a strike.

Box 3.3   Ahmed's critical narrative study 2

Ahmed went to see his dissertation supervisor, Dr Padraig Maguire.

Ahmed explained his idea of analysing the causes and consequences of the strike at the warehouses of the online retailer, using theories about industrial resistance by employees from a critical realist position. Padraig said that the general idea sounded fine, but asked whether Ahmed could express that general idea as a question. Ahmed answered yes, but when Padraig said nothing in response, Ahmed realized that Padraig was expecting him to express it as a question there and then. Ahmed thought for a few moments in silence and then said: 'How does a critical realist analysis help us to understand how workers' resistance to working conditions manifested in a strike and led to changes at an online retailer company's warehouses?' Padraig said that it was a long question, but its strength was that it captured all dimensions of what Ahmed wanted to explore, so that was useful. Padraig recommended that Ahmed keep that question in the forefront of his mind throughout the research for the project, to ensure that his collection of evidence focused on material that would be useful.

Padraig then asked Ahmed a series of questions which Ahmed struggled to answer. Padraig asked why it was important to look at this case, and whether any findings by Ahmed might provide insights for elsewhere. Ahmed had no idea. Padraig said that Ahmed was conducting a case study, and he recommended that Ahmed looked at Lee and Saunders's (2017, 2019) work on case studies as a means both to justify his choice of case study and to look at ways of theorizing when studying only one case. Padraig then asked Ahmed how he was going to order the sequence of events. Ahmed responded: by date order. Padraig said that while chronological sequencing was sensible, it might become cumbersome to organize every piece of evidence by the exact date order, and he recommended that Ahmed look at the idea of temporal bracketing in Langley's (1999) work on theorizing from process data. Padraig asked Ahmed what the sources were he was going to gather evidence from. Ahmed said that he would use a search engine to look for newspaper reports about the company and the strike, and he would go forward from there. This concerned Padraig, as he was not sure that this would be sufficient. Padraig therefore set up a meeting for the following week, and told Ahmed that before that time, he wanted him to:

- justify his choice of case and come up with an explanation of how he might theorize from it;
- propose a less cumbersome method of how he was going to organize the sequence of events;

- identify the full range of sources from which evidence was going to be gathered; and
- prepare a tool for recording the information as it was collected.

The story of Ahmed's study continues in Box 4.6 in Chapter 4.

Constitutive discourse

What does each document represent?

Researchers who combine a constructivist ontology with an interpretive epistemology see individuals interpreting the words and actions of others as symbols that have meanings to which they respond according to those interpretations, helping to construct reality. In this sense, documents may be perceived as representing beliefs and intentions, providing messages from the authors that are used to influence others' behaviours. This can be seen in a range of documents. For example, newspapers provide accounts of incidents that the authors expect the reader to accept as authoritative, and to then act as if that account is accurate and true. Organizations provide policy documents for their employees and others, expecting that those employees will interpret the policies in a particular way and act accordingly. Lecturers provide reading lists, anticipating that their students will interpret that they are to obtain the readings on the lists and spend their time studying them. Doctors provide prescriptions which they anticipate will influence what a patient and a pharmacist will do with that prescription subsequently. Readers write letters to newspapers, seeking to influence others of their opinions. In this sense, the documents are the conveyors of meanings. So the documents that are to be collected will be those which represent an author's intentions and the recipient's actions on receipt of the discourse in the documentation.

How to perceive and justify

The contents of a document are perceived as providing symbols that an author hopes a recipient will act upon. The research questions will indicate both the content of the discourse that is perceived to be influencing another, and the resultant behaviour of another that has been influenced. The justification for the collection of any documents should be that they provide evidence either of the discourse or of the behaviour influenced by the discourse. It may be that the research question is much more limited, and asks about the use of particular devices such as textual rhetoric or images that an author uses to influence others' behaviour. In this case, the use of such devices in an author's discourse will provide the justification for their inclusion.

How to select the documents

As indicated above, the documents to be collected will be those that represent an author's discourse or those that show the resultant actions of others. Thus, in defining what documents to collect, it makes sense when deciding upon a research question to investigate, for the researcher to identify: (1) the author, which could be an individual or collective such as an organization; (2) the recipient, which could be either an intended recipient such as an employee of an organization, or an unintended recipient such as the police being provided with documentary evidence of a fraud; (3) the purpose for which the document is to be put; and (4) the genre of document that is to be collected. This will enable a search – possibly through the internet – of authors, recipients and genres of documents to establish whether they are available in sufficient numbers to address the research question. The researcher will also need to prepare a tool for recording empirical evidence as it is collected. An illustration of this will be elaborated in Chapter 4.

Ultimate purpose

The objective in looking at documents is to examine how they influence behaviour. The behaviour may be assumed from evidence that it exists, or it may be that the behaviour is an outcome that was not intended, but which has been shaped by the discourse represented in the documents, such as when an ultimatum issued in a document precipitates a response of resistance rather than the compliance which was sought. It is important to define an outcome as either desired or undesired, and then show how the messages conveyed in the documents helped to construct it. Let us return to the story of Miao in Box 3.4, who wants to study how different approaches to teaching have been influenced by particular philosophical discourses, which illustrates some of the points above.

Box 3.4   Miao's study of the constitutive quality of documents 2

When Miao explained to Professor Edward Stafford her idea of a dissertation topic of examining whether module content could be seen as constructed from philosophical positions utilized by lecturers, he seemed a little ambivalent. He said that it was an interesting idea and one that could make a good dissertation topic, but he said that the first thing that Miao had to do immediately after their meeting was to contact whichever lecturers' modules Miao might want to use in her dissertation, to explain what she might be doing and to seek their permission in advance. Edward said that Miao had to do this even before she applied for formal ethical approval. Edward asked Miao which modules she was thinking of using and she replied Tony Jones's 'Marketers' Toolbox', Karen Gooding's 'International Marketing' and Alison Owen's 'Green Marketing'. Edward felt a little relieved. As head of his school's Marketing Division, Edward knew that some of his colleagues might be suspicious about why one of his dissertation students might wish to analyse the content of their modules, but Tony, Karen and Alison generally accepted that proposals did not have subterranean motives. Edward made a note to check with them that they would be happy with the study, independently of Miao's approach.

Professor Stafford asked Miao to explain her idea in more detail so that he could assess its authenticity. Miao explained that she thought that without any sort of meaning that can be attached to them, voices are just noises and similarly without any meaning attached to them, words on a slide are just squiggly lines and pictures are just collections of colours. But when meanings are attached, voices can convey sentences, slides are able to convey summary points and pictures may illustrate those summary points. Even in a lecture, where interactions may be minimal, there may be several sets of meanings in operation. There will be that of the lecturer leading the session, and another for each of the students. She said that both the sentences expressed in the voices and the contents of lecture slides may be perceived as sets of meanings that represent a philosophical standpoint. It does not necessarily have to be that of the lecturer – although it could be – but it will express the philosophical stance of either original authors or lecturers. What Miao wanted to do was to assess the extent to which each lecturer's slides represent a particular philosophical position. Miao explained what her initial impressions were of the respective philosophical positions inform-ing Tony Jones's 'Marketers' Toolbox', Karen Gooding's 'International Marketing' and Alison Owen's 'Green Marketing' modules.

Edward agreed that Miao's idea might produce a good dissertation, and said that in addition to approaching the three lecturers to see whether they were willing for her to use their materials in her dissertation, he would like her to complete the following tasks in preparation for their next meeting.

1.   Formulate her research question in a clear and unambiguous way.
2.   Identify the literature that her research would contribute to.
3.   Decide exactly what evidence she needed to gather to answer that question.
4.   Draft an application for ethical approval of her research, to include whether the lecturers had agreed to using their materials.
5.   Prepare a way of recording the information as she collected it to explore the validity of her ideas.

The story of Miao's study continues in Box 4.8 in Chapter 4.

Summary

The purpose of this chapter has been to discuss how to prepare for a study based on documentary evidence. It has used the four different types of approach that have different philosophical underpinnings outlined in Chapter 2, which may be organized to collect documentary evidence, and it has introduced a number of tools that may be useful. The approaches have been illustrated using the examples of the four fictional students from earlier in the book. Having introduced the tools that might be used in different approaches, the book now turns to elaborate the actual appli-cation of those tools in more detail.

4 Collection and compilation of text in documentary research

The objectives of this chapter are to:

- show how to collect and compile the evidence in a study based on a survey of a population using a particular type of document;
- show how to collect and compile the evidence for comparative case studies using a range of different types of documents;
- show how to collect and compile evidence from documents to provide a critical narrative;
- show how to collect and compile evidence from documents to illustrate a constitutive discourse.

Introduction

This chapter shows you how to conduct studies with the research approaches identified hitherto, using only documents that are readily available via the internet. All four of the approaches – a positivist survey, interpretive comparative case studies, a critical narrative and a constitutive discourse – will be illustrated. The discussion will proceed by showing how to operationalize the process of collecting documents in each of these respective approaches to the collection of evidence in turn, starting with the positivist survey. The progress of the different students encountered earlier will be used for illustration in the discussion.

Collecting documents for a positivist survey

When deciding to conduct a survey of documents, it is important to know in advance the research hypotheses that are to be examined through utilization of the evidence contained in the documents that are to be collected, and any inferences for claims about the applicability of the findings from that survey to other instances. It is thus necessary to conduct a literature review first, to identify what is already known about a phenomenon and the population(s) to which that knowledge is applicable, so that what is not known may be added as a research hypothesis, or new populations may be added to those which the phenomenon is currently deemed applicable to. When defining the population to be studied, it is also important to decide on the unit of analysis. For example, although an investigation in the business and management field may be concerned with companies, it may be that there is a better unit of analysis than the company as a whole, either because of the nature of the research hypothesis, or because of the availability of the evidence. For example, if the hypotheses relate to a particular type of policy or function such as the human resource management function, it may be most applicable to define the policy or function as the unit of analysis. Alternatively, if the main source of information is going to be the statement of the chairman/chairwoman in the financial report, the unit of analysis could be the chairman/chairwoman and the hypotheses could be adapted to reflect this.

Once the population to be studied has been identified, it is necessary to make a provisional decision of either studying the entire population or studying only a sample. This decision is likely to be dependent on two factors: firstly, the actual size of the population intimated by your research hypotheses; and secondly, how readily available the documents are for the population as a whole and particular sub-sections of that population. Put simply, the larger the size of the population, the more sensible it is to study just a sample of that population; and the less readily available are the documents containing the evidence that you need to address your research questions, the more likely it is that you will conduct some form of sampling. When choosing which units to study, a technique that allows selection of a representative sample should be used if the aim is to make claims about how the findings from the study relate to the population as a whole. One way of selecting a simple random sample is by numbering each unit in a population, then using the random number generator in a spreadsheet to select a minimum sample of 300. An alternative method, after numbering each unit in the population and choosing your sample size (of preferably a minimum of 300), is to decide on which way to read a random number table, that may be found in some textbooks on statistics or research methods: left to right or vice versa, or up or down and vice versa. You then pick one number with which to start and travel in your pre-chosen direction, selecting units in the interval of the population as a whole that matches the interval with which you reach numbers in the random number table that have three numbers at the end that fall between 1 and 300 (if this is the limit you choose) until you have selected 300 units from the population, which then form a representative sample. It may be that you wish to focus your attention on only part of a population, or it is only possible to get documentary evidence from part of the population. In these cases, it makes sense either to define that part of the population as the whole population, or to stratify the population and select the sample at random from those sub-sections from which documentary evidence may be obtained, but to explain in your methodology chapter what you have done.

We now return to the story of Nnamdi in Box 4.1 for illustration, by reporting how he defined his research hypotheses, chose the population to study to test his hypotheses, and decided how he would identify members of that population.

Box 4.1   Nnamdi's survey 3

Nnamdi looked at the list of things he agreed to do when he first met with Professor Right. These were: (1) review the literature; (2) formulate clearly stated hypotheses that take account of knowledge already known in the literature; (3) define the population to be studied and justify his selection of that population; (4) report on the sources of information that he would collect to test the hypotheses; and (5) prepare a tool for recording the information that he collected. Nnamdi had reviewed the literature on the respective influence of chief executive officer (CEO) performance and corporate social responsibility on corporate financial performance, and he was pleased to see that no academic study had reported specifically on the impact of the respective factors in a slow-growing economy, which he was going to address. Consequently, he formulated the following hypotheses:

- At times of slow economic growth of 1 per cent or less in national gross domestic product (GDP), an organization's financial performance is positively correlated with good performance of the CEO and/or other directors.

- At times of slow economic growth of 1 per cent or less in national GDP, an organization's financial performance is negatively correlated with good performance of the CEO and/or other directors.
- At times of slow economic growth of 1 per cent or less in national GDP, an organization's financial performance is positively correlated with having strong and clearly stated corporate social responsibility policies.
- At times of slow economic growth of 1 per cent or less in national GDP, an organization's financial performance is negatively correlated with having strong and clearly stated corporate social responsibility policies.

Nnamdi decided that the population to be studied would be the FTSE 100 companies. He reasoned that he would be able to get information about these organizations more easily, and that he would be able to obtain a list of such companies from the *Financial Times*. Nnamdi was aware that some industrial sectors were more sensitive than others to downturns in the economy and so he decided also to collect and record information about the sector in which each corporation operated in case the sector was important, so he could identify good and bad performers in each sector. He considered using Nomenclature des Activités Économiques dans la Communauté Européenne (NACE) or North American Industry Classification System (NAICS) codes but he decided instead that he would use Standard Industrial Classification (SIC) codes to organize them according to industry from a British government website (https://assets.publishing.service.gov.uk/government/uploads/system/uploads/attachment_data/file/527619/SIC07_CH_condensed_list_en.csv/preview). He decided to have a break before thinking about the sources of information to collect, and how to record that information when collecting it.

Nnamdi's story continues in Box 4.2.

In a study based on documents, once the research hypotheses have been defined and the population from where the information may be gathered to address those hypotheses has been identified, it is necessary to identify the type of document that is likely to contain the information. Many studies in the business and management field are about companies. An important source of information about companies is their respective websites. The respective websites will not only include details about the organization's product range and operations, but they may also have a stock of, generally positive, new stories and – when companies are listed on a stock market – the annual financial report, any social reports that are produced and details of any philanthropic activities in which they are involved. The annual financial report is an important source of information, as in addition to details about the assets and liabilities of the organization and its financial performance over the preceding 12 months, it contains considerable additional information, including:

- details of its business model, strategy and the environment in which it operates;
- a statement on environmental issues such as emissions;
- reports on human resource issues such as directors' remuneration, employment policy regarding people with disabilities and gender diversity across all areas of the organization; and:
- governance issues, including statements of directors' interests, the conduct of the annual general meeting, board and committees' responsibilities and compliance with the United Kingdom's (UK) Corporate Governance Code.

Although the annual financial report may be an important source of the information about a company, it may not be the only source that is important for a cross-sectional survey. As intimated in Box 4.1, if distinctions between companies in different sectors are significant, an important useful document for classifying companies is a list of standard industrial codes. As we also saw in Box 4.1, Nnamdi intended to collect information about the companies that he was surveying from sources additional to the companies' websites. How he proceeded with this is reported in Box 4.2.

Box 4.2   Nnamdi's survey 4

Nnamdi always found that Italian coffee cleared his mind. Now he felt refreshed and ready to think about the sources of information. He thought that he could get the financial information easily from each organization's audited annual financial reports. Nnamdi would read through the remainder of each report, paying particular attention to the chairperson's report, the reports of other directors including the

CEO, and any report covering strategic issues to identify either positive or negative comments about directors' performance. Nnamdi had followed Professor Right's advice and looked at attribution theory and anticipated that he might not find any self-criticism by directors in annual reports, so he decided to also use a search engine to look for articles in the previous year that might comment on directors' performance, using the name of the company and different descriptions of directors, including specific titles such as chairperson, chairman, chairwoman, chief executive officer and chief financial officer. Nnamdi decided that he would collect information about the corporate social responsibility report by looking at discussions about corporate governance, gender and ethnic balance of directors and the workforce, reports on emissions, considerations of working conditions and child labour in all parts of their supply chains, and discussions of charitable and philanthropic work. Nnamdi also decided that when he was visiting the website of each corporation, he would see whether they produced separate corporate social responsibility reports, and look to see whether the issues that he had identified were evident in those reports. Nnamdi thought that corporations might not necessarily report on outcomes that were not socially responsible, so he decided that when he was using the search engine for articles that commented on the directors' performance, he would also combine the name of the company with a range of terms – such as 'redundancies', 'spillages', 'exploitation' – that indicated violation of social responsibility.

Nnamdi decided to take another break before deciding on how he would record the information.

Nnamdi's story continues in Box 4.3.

When collecting documents, we might want to record this information in a way that will allow easier analysis at a subsequent stage. For example, let us assume that our research hypothesis aims to explore whether the percentage of female directors affects the percentage increase in gross profit at an organization. In this instance, the independent variable is the percentage of female directors, and the dependent variable is the percentage change in profit. A moderating variable may be the sector in which the organization operates. It may also be that independent evidence is sought from another source to confirm that female directors play a meaningful role in the functioning of the organization. Having identified the key forms of information to be collected, a recording sheet may be prepared, perhaps using a spreadsheet. The way in which Nnamdi did this is reported in Box 4.3. However, in the example of the relationship between the percentage of female directors and percentage change in profit, the spreadsheet may look similar to Table 4.1.

Box 4.3   Nnamdi's survey 5

As Nnamdi restarted his work, he thought about a couple of things that his research methods lecturer said in the lecture on statistics. Firstly, that it is easy to transfer information from a spreadsheet into the Statistical Package for Social Sciences (IBM SPSS) for easy analysis. So he decided that he would use a spreadsheet to record the information that he collected. Secondly, that items had to be measurable, so even if the evidence being collected started off as qualitative in form, it had to be given a numerical value. Nnamdi reasoned that while the financial information that he collected would have numerical values, most of the other information that he collected would not, so he thought that the best way to proceed was to prepare a coding frame for each piece of information that he collected, relating to his hypothesis. He decided that for the performance of the company directors, he would have codes of: 7 when positive references in the financial accounts were more numerous than negative remarks and the good reports from other sources were greater than bad reports from those sources; 6 if the positive reports of the CEO and other directors' performance were greater than the negative references in the annual accounts and there were no good or bad reports in the other sources; 5 when the good reports in the financial accounts were more numerous than the bad reports, but the bad reports from other sources were greater than the good reports from those sources; 4 if there were no reports – either good or bad – about the directors and CEO in both the annual report and in other sources; 3 when the bad reports in the financial accounts were more numerous than the good reports but the good reports from other sources were greater than the bad reports from those sources; 2 if the bad reports of the CEO and other directors' performance were greater than good reports in the financial accounts and there were no good or bad reports in the other sources; and 1 when the bad reports of the CEO and other directors' performance were greater than good reports in the financial accounts and the bad reports from other sources were greater than the good reports from those sources.

Nnamdi decided to use a parallel form of coding for recording information about corporate social responsibility in his spreadsheet. For example, he would have the code of 7 for instances where reports of good examples of corporate social responsibility initiatives were greater than reports of violations of corporate social responsibility that appeared in either the organization's financial accounts or in any separate corporate social responsibility accounts performance, and the good reports in other sources were more numerous than the bad reports in those sources.

Nnamdi planned the layout of his spreadsheet for recording the information. He would organize the spreadsheet so that each company in the FTSE 100 would be organized vertically in the first column. Horizontally, the subsequent successive columns in the top line would read: SIC code; pre-tax profit from previous year; pre-tax profit from year in which GDP growth had been 1 per cent; monetary value of change in pre-tax profit; percentage value of change in pre-tax profit; index score for the performance of the CEO and directors; and index score for corporate social responsibility.

Nnamdi was confident that he had completed the five tasks set by Professor Right. He anticipated that Mark Right would ask him how he would analyse the material once it had been collected and he had the answer that he would use IBM SPSS to test the correlative relationships expressed in his hypotheses.

Once the recording sheet is prepared, it is now possible to collect one or two documents of the desired genre – such as the annual report – from the defined population to check that the information is present, and the length of time that it will take to identify the relevant information in the document and record it. This will give some indication of whether it is necessary to revise what one is going to study: that is, the whole population or a sample. This examination of a few documents and the recording of the information may be considered what some authors would describe as a pilot study, although if the information has been collected and recorded successfully, the firms' documents studied will form part of the

Table 4.1   Example of a spreadsheet for recording information

Source(s) of information	Independent variable			Moderating variable	Dependent variable			Independent variable
Firm name	Number of female directors	Total number of directors	Female directors as % of all directors	Industrial sector	Profit in previous year	Profit in current year	% change in profit from previous to current year	Other evidence of female directors' role in organization
Firm A								
Firm B								
Firm C								

main study. At this stage, if it is going to be quicker to download all of the important documents at once, before recording the information, this may be done. Whether you record the information as you download, or download the information and then record, is a matter of choice based on the way in which you wish to organize your work. When recording, it is important to make note of any information that is incomplete and to see if there are other ways of obtaining the information, such as by using a search engine to find this information on the World Wide Web or by emailing the organization. Details of the incomplete information from the initial collection, the steps taken to obtain the information, the extent of success in obtaining the information and the extent to which the information remained incomplete, should be recorded so that the information about completeness may be reported when the study is written up. For example, if it is assumed that the policy of interest is about bonuses paid to directors of FTSE 100 companies and the main source of information is the company's annual financial statement, but the desired information was found in 89 organizations and the remaining 11 were emailed and responses providing the missing information were received from 10, the note made for subsequent inclusion in the methodological chapter may be similar to: 'Information from the FTSE 100 was sought initially from their annual reports for the financial year ending in 2020. This information was found in 89 out of the 100 annual reports. The remaining 11 were emailed and 10 responded providing the requisite information. This left just [name of company] from which the desired information could not be collected during the time period of this study. The extensive coverage of the FTSE 100 provides confidence in the accuracy of the report on policies of directors' bonuses of this classification of organizations'. If you have recorded the information, your evidence will be ready for analysis. Details of how you might conduct your analysis may be found in Dawson (2016) or Scherbaum and Shockley (2015).

Collecting documents for interpretive, comparative case studies

When conducting interpretative, comparative case studies, it is necessary to review the literature, generate research questions and design the research for collection of documents to generate answers to your research questions. Some authors indicate that it is desirable to plan case studies only after conducting an extensive review of the literature and defining ultimate research questions in advance before executing the conduct of the research (e.g., Yin, 2018). However, it is sensible to acknowledge that this is not necessarily always possible, so when deciding to conduct comparative case studies to draw out different people's interpretations of their experiences from documentary research, it may be that the relationship that you are going to examine is less rigidly specified than would be the case if you were stating research hypotheses for a quantitative survey. Nevertheless, it is useful to have some idea of different literatures in which your cases may fit, and the way in which differences in the case studies may provide answers to the research questions. Thus, although the research may start with a general empirical observation, the development of the research questions, the reading of academic literature and the collection of further empirical evidence may take place iteratively. Lee and Saunders (2017) use the term 'emergent' to describe cases that are developed through this type of process. As noted above, the type of logic employed in this form of research is abductive. To help your reader understand the process of research and to demonstrate that you have been systematic in your approach, it is important to document how you developed your research questions and proceeded with your research.

For example, let us assume that when visiting your local independent convenience shop, you note how the store has branded a number of products, including bleach, as essential household goods to prevent the spread of COVID-19. You are also aware that consumers are increasingly sensitive to the environmental impact of different products. Given the extent of the pandemic, you think that it would be interesting to consider whether other stores have followed the example of this small independent store. You have read some work, such as that by Siu and Wong (2002), which reports that one of the factors that influence consumers' perception of safety is the store where the product is sold. You decide that supermarkets have a national – and sometimes international – reputation that would endorse the perceptions of the safety of the products that they sold, and so it would be useful to examine whether supermarkets are viewing particular cleaning products as helping to prevent COVID-19 contamination. Thus, the initial definition of the case is instances of supermarkets' marketing of cleaning products. You also know that you and your peers try to purchase environmentally friendly products. You then start to review the literature, including Joshi and Rahman (2015), that confirms consumers' desire for environmentally friendly products and marketers' catering to those desires. You hear on the news how the reproduction rate of COVID-19 has regional variations, and that leads you to develop research questions that link issues of supermarkets' perceptions of strengths of different products and their marketing campaigns to the regional concentration, type of store and pattern of ownership. After preparing a recording sheet that shows the background of the supermarket, you are now in a position to visit their websites and examine their marketing campaigns to address your research questions. Throughout the period that you are conducting your research, it is likely that you will continue to review the literature, to give you additional ideas of how you may interpret your evidence when you analyse it. The way that you might record your collection of evidence as part of a broader process is shown in Table 4.2. Documenting the steps that you have taken in this way, from the initial observation that led you to think about what you should research, through to the execution of the research, will help to convince the reader that you have prepared your dissertation in a systematic way, even though you have not defined your research questions solely from the literature in the way that positivist, quantitative surveys are conducted.

This example conveys the seamless process between reviewing the literature, identifying a problem for study, defining the scope of the study in terms of the units of analysis or cases, and deciding on the research strategy and initial design of research tools such as recording sheets that are often involved when conducting comparative case studies, before and while empirical evidence is collected. We can see a similar process as we return to Simone's research reported in Box 4.4, who started with an empirical observation from her own vacation and was then asked to

Table 4.2   Documentation of development of research ideas and
               strategy

Stage in research	Action
Made initial empirical observation	Noted marketing of cleaning products at local shop
Reflected on literature read previously	Recalled that perceived safety of product is linked to the store where the product is purchased
Defined the type of cases to study, based on initial empirical observation and previous reading	Articulated case as supermarkets' instances of marketing cleaning products as capability to counter COVID-19 contamination
Made nascent comparison with an original empirical observation and a further empirical observation	Noted that consumers also have concerns about the environmental impact
Ongoing literature review	Read literature on consumers' desires for environmentally friendly products
Additional empirical observation.	Noted that the recorded reproduction rate of COVID-19 varies regionally
Definition of research questions	Are supermarkets likely to view the marketing strength of cleaning products as countering infection by COVID-19 differently according to their regional concentration?
Design of research	1. use internet research to distinguish between supermarkets based on regional concentration, typical size of store and country where owners are based; 2. identify regional variation of rates of reproduction of COVID-19 from the Government's Office for National Statistics website; 3. prepare a recording sheet identifying characteristics of supermarket from point 1 above, and evidence of any campaign; 4. visit websites of major supermarkets to see whether they have headlines that relate to either the merits of products in addressing COVID-19, environmental-friendliness of products, or any other regular campaign, such as seasonal or return-to-school.
Execute research	Collect and record information
Ongoing literature review	Reading to identify marketing issues identified in the literature

revise her research questions by her dissertation supervisor. What should be clear from both examples is the necessity to prepare an appropriate recording sheet that reflects the nature of the research questions that have been formulated, and then to visit websites that permit the collection of documents that provide evidence of differences in opinion between different cases. In the examples provided, this has been either by visiting organizations of the same type to identify differences in their priorities and presentations, or by visiting user feedback sites. There are a range of different consumer, employee and community feedback websites in the public domain that provide information which captures differences in opinion, including *Indeed*, *MyBuilder*, *Tripadvisor* and *Trustpilot*. More details of these different websites are found in the Appendix. Depending on the research questions, other sources of documents that may provide insights into differences of opinion around particular events include letters to newspapers; regular columnists in newspapers which could include lifestyle, political or sports commentators; or magazines that include reader-authored human interest stories.

Box 4.4   Simone's interpretative study 3

Simone looked at her notes from her meeting with Tina and saw that she was asked to do the following:

1.   Develop refined research questions.
2.   Identify the documentary sources from which she could collect the information to address her research questions.
3.   Prepare a tool for recording the information that was collected and necessary to answer the refined research questions in ways that would make the analysis easier.

Simone thought about her general research question, of what influences people's experience of their holidays when staying at hotels in the UK. She realized that with the information that she now intended to gather, she could ask more specific questions, and she wrote down the following:

1.   How does the unit in which someone travels – of being alone, part of a couple or a family group – affect people's experiences of their holidays at hotels in the UK?

2. How does the weather while holidaying affect people's experience of their holidays at hotels in the UK?
3. How does the location of the hotel – in the countryside, on the coast or in a city – affect people's experience of their holidays at hotels in the UK?
4. How do the facilities of the hotel affect people's experience of their holidays at hotels in the UK?

Satisfied with her more detailed refined questions, Simone reflected on the second task and realized that she had already identified a directory of hotels at https://www.britinfo.net/hotels/ from which to choose the ones to study, she knew the ability of the Met Office to provide details of the daily weather in different locations, each hotel's website provided details of its facilities, and *Tripadvisor* provided accounts of what different travellers thought of the hotels where they stayed. All that she needed to do now was to prepare a tool for the collection of the information in an order that would make the subsequent analysis easier.

Simone decided that she would use a spreadsheet to record the information as she collected it. She would use the spreadsheet to organize material vertically about each hotel, which would have a hidden note about its respective facilities so that she could refer to this quickly when she wanted to, the weather and the unit for travel, which she would expand vertically for each comment made by someone on the *Tripadvisor*

		Sun	Mon	Tues	Wed	Thurs	Fri	Sat
Hotel 1	Weather	21°C / Rain	24°C / Sun	25°C / Sun	18°C / Cloud	17°C / Rain	17°C / Rain	23°C / Sun
	Unit for travel							
	Couple	Quote						
	Family	Quote						
	Family			Quote				
	Lone				Quote			
	Couple							Quote
Hotel 2	Weather	24°C / Sun	26°C / Sun	2°C / Sun	17°C / Cloud	17°C / Rain	17°C / Rain	25°C / Sun
	Unit for travel							
	Lone	Quote						
	Couple	Quote						

site. She would organize the horizontal axis by the day of the week when the comments were recorded. Simone anticipated that she would have six weeks to collect empirical evidence. She decided that she would record all of the information on a single sheet so that she could review the information easily. She decided to lay out a week's record to show Tina at their next meeting, and prepared the table above.

Simone's story continues in Box 4.5.

The illustration reported above relating to supermarkets' perceptions and marketing of the strengths of different products highlights how it may be difficult to decide when to make an application for ethical approval, as initial empirical observations were made quite inadvertently. Chapter 3 reported that ethical approval procedures are likely to vary between different institutions, and it is important to seek the advice of your dissertation supervisor or another member of the academic staff, but it is important to gain that approval before embarking on the main part of your study, as done by Simone and reported in Box 4.5. As some institutions do not permit collection of any evidence without ethical approval and may rule that information is not permissible as part of the dissertation, it is always sensible to go back and confirm any early empirical observations that were made before ethical approval was granted, after you have gained ethical approval. That will provide assurances that all the material that you have gathered may be used in your dissertation.

Box 4.5   Simone's interpretative study 4

Simone met with Tina, who was very pleased with what Simone had prepared. Tina asked Simone how she intended to proceed now. Simone said that first she was going to complete an application for ethical approval, and continue with her reading to expand the literature review on issues relating to the influence of weather, location, facilities and unit of travel on people's experience of leisure activities, every day. Once she had ethical approval, in addition to continuing with her reviewing of the literature, she would visit both the Met Office website to record the weather at the locations where her hotels were situated, and the *Tripadvisor* web pages of the hotels to record any reviews over the next six weeks. Tina asked Simone how she would know when the reviewers had stayed at the hotel. Simone acknowledged that it would be impossible to be sure, but she would assume that it was in the week previously, unless it was stated more explicitly or their quotes provided evidence that Simone could align with other information that she collected, such as mention of the weather. Tina agreed that was a good strategy. Tina advised Simone to write down details of this decision and everything about her method to date, to report in her methodology chapter when she came to write it. Tina asked Simone how she intended to analyse the information once the six weeks of evidence had been collected. Simone said that she did not know yet. Tina suggested that as Simone was interested in people's experiences, she might consider using template analysis and use the unit in which the traveller holidayed as the primary codes, location of hotel as secondary codes, hotel facilities as tertiary codes, and different types of weather as quaternary codes. She recommended that Simone looked at King and Brooks's (2017) book on *Template Analysis* for further guidance.

Collecting documents for a critical narrative study

In some ways, a critical narrative study may also be considered as a case study, as it will be a narrative of a particular event or phenomenon. In this regard, some of the discussion in the previous section – although not that about comparisons – also applies to critical narratives. Collecting documents to conduct a narrative study of an event is most sensible when the event has been written about from the perspective of some parties, but not from the stance of others. Such a scenario lends itself to asking research questions such as: 'How did [*a particular party*] view or influence [*such-and-such event*]?' Once the event has been chosen, the research question may be refined by building in a particular theoretical account. For example, it may be that a researcher wishes to understand how car component manufacturers came to be involved in preferred supplier relationships with a major car manufacturer, and believes that it may be attributable to the ways in which executives in the motor car industry move between different companies in that sector. Thus, a research question might be: 'How has the movement of executives between companies in the motor manufacturing sector contributed to preferred supplier relationships: an actor-network analysis?' It is often suggested that any study should seek to address two questions. The first is 'Why did something happen?' In the question that is posed here we can see evidence of a 'why' question as the exploration is about the contribution of executives' occupational mobility to the development of preferred-supplier relationships in the motor car industry. The second question that it is often suggested that a project should address is: 'So what?' It is possible to express this second question as: 'Why is it important for the reader to know this?' This research question might be considered more worthy if preferred-supplier relationships had proved to be either extremely useful or extremely dysfunctional in a particular industry, and such a justification was used when explaining the reason for the study. If a narrative study has been written from the perspective of one party involved in an event, but not from that of another, the partial nature of existing knowledge could also be used to justify the study.

In considering how to collect documents for a critical narrative study, it is useful to reflect on Pentland's (1999, pp. 712-713) suggestions of the different components of a narrative. These are as follows.

Chronological sequence

There must be a temporal or chronological sequence in the account of the event, including a clear beginning, a middle and an end. Thus, a first stage in preparing for the collection of documents may be to define the parameters of the sequence in terms of the start date and end date. The phenomenon to be studied is likely to have developed over time, or to have changed over time. It is thus important to establish both the sequence of the events and the timeline over which those events occur. One way of organizing the sequence and the timeline is through chronometric time. Chronometric time permits events' measurement by periods of equal length such as minutes, hours, days and weeks. However, it is important to recognize that when seeking to understand the course of events or a process, chronometric time is not necessarily the best measure. Often, events may be planned over a long period, implemented slowly and then suddenly come to fruition with a number of either immediate effects, or consequences that only materialize over a longer term. If the important part of the process relates to developments over a period that does not progress in exact parallel with chronological time, an important tool or concept for defining a timeline is what Langley (1999) defines as temporal bracketing.

The concept of temporal bracketing allows organization of a sequence according to the most important stages in a phenomenon, largely independently of the framework imposed by chronometric time. For example, it may be that an organization has defined a policy, which is followed by industrial action, and the industrial action then leads to the policy being changed in some way. This may be illustrated by a dispute over university lecturers' pensions in 2018-20 when the administrators of the Universities Superannuation Scheme (USS) in the UK decided that it could no longer provide pensions at a given level for the contributions that lecturers were paying towards their pensions. The University and College Union (UCU) organized industrial action in 2018 and, following that action, the administrators of the USS scheme agreed to review their earlier changes. However, the proposed revisions were considered to be too minor and further industrial action followed late in 2019 and in the early months of 2020. Appropriate temporal brackets in this scenario might be: the period prior to the proposed change to pensions; the period of the proposed changes; the initial industrial action in 2018; the period of the promised review; the subsequent industrial action; and the period following the subsequent industrial action. The temporal bracketed timeline could provide the basic framework for the recording sheet when collecting documents.

Focal actor or actors

The second component of a narrative that Pentland identifies is the focal actor or focal actors. Narratives will always have a subject, regardless of whether that subject is someone or something. There is likely to be one or more protagonists who are central figures in the narrative and there may also be an opponent or antagonist of the protagonists. Such characters may not be referred to by name. There may also be a number of more peripheral characters. The sequence of activities involving the central figures of the protagonist(s) and the antagonist(s) will provide a thread that integrates the characters and events to form the narrative, which may be considered as comparable with the plot of a story. Thus, when developing the recording sheet for referencing the collection of documents, it can be useful to have the temporal brackets down the vertical axis and the main characters along the horizontal axis, to help show where an abundance of information has been collected and where an insufficient amount of material has been gathered and more is required.

Narrator

The third component of a narrative that Pentland identifies is a narrator, who expresses the narrative. The narrator could be the protagonist, although this would be partially dependent on whether there is simply one key protagonist. If the objective is to realize what Brown and Humphreys (2002) have described as polyphonic – as distinct from monophonic – accounts where different voices are heard in the narrative, it may be sensible to prepare the critical narrative from the perspective of a separate narrator. The way in which the narrative is narrated is a decision that may be deferred until after the documentary evidence has been collected.

Canonical frame of reference

A factor that will also influence the choice of the narrator is Pentland's (1999) fourth component of a narrative, and that is its canonical frame of reference, which will express the values or morals of the narrator and the narrative. It is the expression of the morals – found in dichotomous categories of good and bad, right and wrong, appropriate and inappropriate, and so on – that helps to distinguish a simple record of events from a narrative. That expression of morals provides the sense of meaning for the narrative, and sets the standards in an implicit invitation for the reader to judge the actions of the protagonists, antagonists and other characters in the narrative. Some theoretical frameworks, such as agency theory or Marxism, will – if they are adopted – inform the content of the morals and help the reader to decide with whom their sympathies are to lie in the particular events that appear in the narrative. In using a theoretical framework to inform the morality of the narrative, there are likely to be some expectations of consistency in applying the morality from the framework throughout the narrative. In preparing the recording sheet for the collection of documents, it is sensible to include a heading along the horizontal axis that permits either a comment or recording of further articles that comment on the ethics of the events from the protagonist's and others' viewpoints.

Context

The fifth and final component of Pentland's ideas around narratives is the provision of information about context. While the narrative will be a moral story about the sequence of events that affect particular protagonists and antagonists, the author of the narrative should use different textual devices to indicate the characteristics of the protagonists and antagonists, the conditions under which they make decisions, the timing of those decisions, and so on. Cues around these events may also be included in the recording sheet alongside the comments about the morality of actions.

The issues of identifying a research question, deciding on the timeline, the protagonists and antagonists, the theoretical stance and the context and initial considerations of the recording sheet, are illustrated in the case of Ahmed that we return to in Box 4.6.

Box 4.6   Ahmed's critical narrative study 3

Following Dr Maguire's advice, Ahmed read through Lee and Saunders (2017) and thought that he could justify the case of the strike at the warehouses of the online retailer on the basis that it was a politically important case. There had been press stories of stressful working conditions at the warehouses of other online retailers, but to Ahmed's knowledge, this was the biggest online retailer. Furthermore, to Ahmed's knowledge, there had not previously been any nationwide industrial action taken at other online retailers, or at this company. Previously, forms of resistance were generally manifest in individual actions such as absenteeism or resignations. The size of the organization and the nationwide nature of the collective action made this a politically important case. Ahmed thought that as he was justifying the selection of his case for its political importance, he should adopt a particularization approach to theorizing about the case by providing an explanation of why the industrial action at the case organization materialized in the way that it did. Ahmed thought that he could also propose an analytic or theoretical generalization that, if the same conditions as those found at the warehouses of the online retailer prior to the industrial actions were also to materialize at other large online retailers, they could also precipitate collective industrial action.

Having addressed the first task Padraig Maguire had set, Ahmed read through Langley's (1999) article and thought that it would be most useful to use Langley's idea of temporal bracketing. Ahmed thought that he could organize any evidence that he collected into the period prior to the strike which could be divided into the immediate two months before the strike and the entire period before those two months, the period of the strike industrial action, the first two months after the strike, and the period since those two months. Ahmed thought the third task that Padraig had set him might be the hardest challenge, judging by what his supervisor said. So he started by entering the name of the organization and the words 'strike' and 'working conditions' into a search engine. In addition to a whole succession of newspaper articles and other press reports, the initial search led Ahmed to the *Indeed* site (at https://www.indeed.co.uk/), where he found more than 60 000 comments by people who had worked previously at the organization, on what they thought of their erstwhile employer. He was also very pleased to see that the comments had a date registered for when each was made, so he would be able to organize them into his temporal brackets to see how things changed between before and after the industrial action. Ahmed was excited by the availability of such information, and after looking through the comments to see that some were provided by delivery drivers and clerical workers – which he decided to exclude – Ahmed took a rest while he considered the last task that Padraig had set for him: of development of an appropriate tool for recording the information.

The story of Ahmed's study continues in Box 4.7.

Once a recording sheet is prepared, it is possible to collect the information about a particular event. Depending on the nature of the sequence of events to be covered by the narrative, some details may be found on some of the review websites identified previously, as illustrated by Ahmed's use of the *Indeed* website in Box 4.6. However, as a narrative is about a sequence of events, it may be that the best possible source of information about that sequence is to be found in newspaper accounts. It is sensible to use a general database to identify newspaper articles about an event. NewsBank and British Newspaper Archive facilities are available for this purpose through many university libraries. As a means of double-checking that all information has been collected, it is also sensible to check the indexes of national newspapers for the period covering the sequence of events. For the period over which the events took place, it may also be useful to check the letters pages of those newspapers. If the events occurred in a specific geographic area – even if they had national or international significance – it is of value to check the local media to see whether local newspapers covered the event. There are a number of sites that provide a directory of the local media covering outlets in different regions, including that of Local Media Works (which may be found at http://www.localmediauk.org/A-Z-Newsbrands?). Once the different sources of information have been identified and ethical approval sought, it is possible to progress to collecting the information, as is the case in Ahmed's study shown in Box 4.7.

Box 4.7   Ahmed's critical narrative study 4

Ahmed decided that he would organize the sheet for recording the information as it was collected as a form of matrix. On the vertical axis of the matrix would be the temporal brackets of the longer-term period prior to the industrial action, the two months immediately prior to the commencement of the industrial action, the period of the industrial action, the two-month period immediately following the action, and the period from two months after the industrial action. Ahmed looked through some of the material that appeared on the *Indeed* website and he saw that a number of themes recurred in the comments, including salary, physical layout of the workspace, stress related to speed of work, insensitive managers, insufficient time to take scheduled meal breaks because of the time that it took going between the workspace and the canteen, and insecure contracts organized through an agency third party. He decided to have these as headings for themes in the initial

Issues-> / Temporal brackets	Salary	Insecure contracts	Poor layout of workplace and injuries	Work speed	Poor access to facilities	Insensitive management
Longer-term period prior to action						
Two-month period prior to action						
Industrial action						
Two-month period after action						
Period more than two months after the action						

matrix, but he would report – when he met with Dr Maguire – that he would add to those headings as he encountered recurring themes in the comments on the *Indeed* site, or in newspaper coverage of the company. Ahmed decided to prepare the above rudimentary recording sheet to show Dr Maguire what he had in mind.

Ahmed was satisfied that he had addressed all of the issues that Padraig had asked him to consider in preparation for their meeting, and that he had a way of seeing how the industrial action had led to changes in the reality at the online retail organization's warehouses.

When they met, Padraig Maguire was delighted with Ahmed's progress and impressed by his discovery of the *Indeed* website, which Padraig thought might be useful for his own research. He told Ahmed to fill in the form seeking ethical clearance, and to wait for confirmation of that clearance before collecting the evidence.

Collection of documentary evidence for a constitutive discourse study

There are a number of areas of everyday and organizational life where there are expectations that the expression of ideas will shape subsequent behaviour. These range from prohibitions in laws, rules and regulations that are designed to govern citizens' behaviour; to prescriptions of medicines and treatments for people deemed to be in ill-health that affect how patients are treated; the assimilation of religious beliefs from different scriptures that influence definitions and adoption of moral behaviours; the provisions of budgets and strategies within organizations and the advertisements of products that affect how organizations and their customers may function; and the recording of witnesses to a committee or in a court case that may influence both the decisions taken by that committee or court and the actions that follow from those decisions. Yet, although the words may convey intentions, the outcomes – even when influenced by the words – may be different to what was intended. Thus, if one wishes to use documents for a constitutive study, it is important to be able to articulate the contents of the discourse that are deemed to have constitutive powers, and to be able to view the outcome of the discourse being employed, even if that outcome is not exactly as intended. Thus, even though the research may employ an inductive logic where the conclusions are derived principally from what is observed, it does not preclude defining what is the anticipated relationship between the discourse and an anticipated consequence. Similarly, although a study may be inductive, it should always be kept in mind that a dissertation is an academic piece of work, and academic research is expected to contribute to an academic literature. It is thus important that the study is related to an academic literature.

The most obvious areas of academic literature to explore are those that address the content of the discourse that are deemed to have constitutive powers, the constitutive outcome of the discourse, and other studies that are influenced by ideas about the constitutive powers of language. Once the relationship has been decided, in a study that relies on documentary evidence, it is necessary to identify evidence of the discourse that is deemed to have the constitutive power and documentary evidence of the outcome. As indicated above, the existence of laws, rules, regulations, religious scriptures, records of witness statements, and so on, may be relatively easy to obtain. Documentary evidence of the behaviour that they have constituted may be more difficult to acquire. For this reason, it is sometimes easier – particularly when working within the short time period allowed for a dissertation – to start from documentary evidence of the behaviour that has been constituted, and then seek documentary evidence about how language helped to constitute that behaviour. One example might be finding newspaper reports that beauty spots in England found it difficult to manage, safely, the influx of tourists that they experienced when the COVID-19 pandemic lockdown restrictions were eased in the UK, and then finding the documents that detail the nature of the restrictions that were lifted. The issues of formulating research questions in a clear way, identifying a relevant literature and defining the type of documentary evidence that is needed for a successful study, is illustrated in Box 4.8, where we return to Miao's study.

Box 4.8   Miao's study of the constitutive quality of documents 3

Miao was relieved that Tony Jones, Karen Gooding and Alison Owen agreed to allow her to use their materials in her dissertation. They all seemed delighted, and said that they would like to see a copy of the dissertation once it was completed. This pleased Miao. With their approval secured, Miao set about the first task set by Professor Stafford, of formulating a clearly stated research question. She wrote down: 'What philosophical positions are manifest when lecturers in marketing contribute to the construction of knowledge through their lectures?' Miao was happy with that, as it captured her own philosophical position that knowledge was constructed, and it would allow her to examine how others were constructing knowledge in lectures. Miao thought about the literature that she would use when writing up. She thought that it was a very good question for Professor Stafford to ask, because she was not conducting a normal study of a marketing phenomenon, but was looking at the implicit assumptions being made by lecturers in their presentation of information. Miao got in touch with the head librarian responsible for the business and management field, and the librarian said that Miao might find the library section on management education useful and also recommended some journals in the field. While Miao was looking through the library's resources, she also thought that she would look at the section on research methods to inform her design. Miao browsed through some books on reflexivity and discovered that this entailed deep questioning of one's own assumptions and she thought that – as her research was about questioning implicit assumptions – this was another body of literature, in addition to the management education literature, that she could tell Professor Stafford that she would contribute to.

Miao thought about what module materials she might be able to use in her research to address her research question as – in addition to copies of the PowerPoint slides used in lectures – there were audio-recordings of the lectures, tutorial exercises and suggested solutions on the websites. Miao reasoned that the tutorial materials were designed only to reinforce knowledge that had been constructed in the lectures, so there might not be any great benefit in collecting them. She also thought about using the audio-recordings of the lectures, but decided against that because, to some extent, she would simply replicate what was already in the text. She reasoned that as all of the other 300 students who were in the lecture theatre could be considered as participating in the audio-recording, she may need the consent of them all for the lectures that they attended if she was to obtain ethical approval. She decided that made the task far too complex and so she decided to focus on the contents of the lecture slides only. Having decided on the documentary material that she would collect, she then revised her research question to state the following: 'What philosophical positions are manifest in the lecture slides of lecturers in marketing when they contribute to the construction of knowledge in their lectures?' Miao also made a note of key authors – namely Russell (2011), Mannheim (1952, 1954) and Piaget (1955) – of classical texts about the three respective philosophical positions of logical positivism, interpretivism and social constructivism that she would use in the composition of 'ideal types' of logically consistent models (Weber, 1949) of the ideas that she would use to examine whether they were manifest in the slides of her lecturers. Miao decided to write a summary of each of the authors' ideas that she would use to analyse the lecture slides in advance of collection of those slides, so that her deep analysis of the slides did not influence her documentation of the epistemological stances. Now that Miao had decided on the documents that she was going to collect as empirical evidence, she was able to prepare a draft of her application for ethical approval. With that completed, out of the tasks that Edward Stafford had set her, she had only to prepare a way of recording the information to explore the validity of her ideas.

The story of Miao's study continues in Box 4.9.

The story of Miao as reported in Box 4.8 is interesting because of another issue. That is the question of ethics. We all have a number of identities – for example, student, partner, son or daughter, and so on. Indeed, Lee and Aslam (2018) indicate that it is important for a researcher to seek to align the values expressed in the research with the values that are manifest in those other identities if the researcher is not to experience some form of dissonance that could make them feel uncomfortable and unhappy. Ethical procedures of institutions are designed to ensure that protocols that protect people involved in our research are observed. In the illustration provided by Miao, there is a potential conflict emerging between Miao in her identity as simply a student, and Miao in her role as a nascent researcher, conducting an investigation for her dissertation. The potential conflict between these two identities helps to illuminate that it is not only important to observe ethical protocols because they are there, but if Miao wishes to continue to have good student-lecturer relationships with the academics whose modules she is including in her research, she needs to act in an open and transparent way, because it is the right thing to do and failure to do so could be detrimental to her personal relationships with those others.

Once it has been decided what documents are deemed to have constitutive powers and which documents are going to show the new situation, it is useful to produce an appropriate recording sheet. The recording sheet should have a minimum of three columns. The first will represent a description of the 'before' situation. In the illustration from Miao, the need for this was precluded by the historical nature of the key texts, and Miao only asking whether the key texts influenced the contents of the lecture slides in an implicit way. More generally, it may be possible to build a picture of what happened previously based in part on previous knowledge, so it will be useful to collect some documentary evidence that reports on the existence of the situation prior to the application of the constitutive documents along the important criteria where change was experienced. This can be achieved through using key terms and dates in a search engine. Preferably, this column should be completed in advance of searching for the documents to fill the other columns, to help ensure the authenticity of the change that is being claimed. The second column will include details of the documents that are deemed to have constitutive capabilities. The third column will include details of the changed situation. It will be useful to date the time when the documents were produced and the time when the records of the alleged changed situation were created by the witness reporting on the changed situation, to demonstrate that the constitutive qualities assumed about the document do exist. There should be consistent evidence of the change between that which existed prior to the intervention from the documents, the essential qualities of the document and the change that was effected by them. The population of a recording sheet with details about the evidence collected will enable recognition during the process of collection of whether sufficient evidence has been accumulated. It should be noted that lack of supportive evidence does not invalidate the study; it will simply be necessary to describe the objectives, what was done, the absence of conclusive findings, and reflections on why that may be the case. As long as this is done in ways that observe the requirements of your dissertation, there is no reason why your dissertation should not be considered to be successful.

The collection of information to address research questions in documentary studies that investigate the constitutive powers of discourse is illustrated by the continuing story of Miao in Box 4.9.

Box 4.9   Miao's study of the constitutive quality of documents 4

Miao's evidence collection appeared to be relatively easy. After she had prepared the ideal types of the different philosophies and gained ethical approval for her study, she had only to download the lecture slides from the webpages of the respective modules. However, Edward Stafford has asked to prepare a tool for recording the information as she collected it, to make it easy for her to explore the validity of her ideas once the information was collected. Miao decided that she would prepare a sheet with three columns that was each headed by one of the three philosophical positions along the horizontal axis. She decided that she would use a different sheet for each lecture, and as she downloaded each lecture she would paste the slides under the column if the contents of that slide suggested adherence to one or another of the philosophical positions. She developed a sheet providing guidance on how she was to interpret slides, which included such instructions as:

- Prescriptions, formula and unidirectional diagrams = positivist.
- Cultural variations and different pictures representing same concept = interpretive.
- Open-ended questions and abstract pictures = constructivist.

She decided that when she downloaded all of the lectures of all of the lectures, she would use different colour paper – light blue for the 'Marketers' Toolbox', pink for 'International Marketing' and light green for 'Green Marketing' – when printing out the documentary records that showed the evidence that she had collected. Miao anticipated that this would make it easy for her to obtain an initial impression, from the pattern of distribution of slides across the columns of a particular coloured paper, where her original idea had any corroboration and where it did not.

When Miao met with Edward Stafford, he expressed satisfaction with how she had progressed, and although he encouraged her to expand her guidance sheet for how she recorded the slides as she downloaded them, he did say that once she had received ethical approval, she could proceed to her evidence collection stage.

Summary

This chapter has shown how to collect documents when using a research strategy of a survey, comparative cases, a critical narrative and consideration of the constitutive qualities of documents. While all these approaches differ, there are some general issues that were raised in this chapter and the previous one to keep in mind, especially when embarking on a dissertation project in a short period. Firstly, be sure of the approach that you wish to adopt at the outset, and conduct an initial review to ensure that the documents are likely to be available to carry out such a study. Secondly, define your research questions or hypotheses as concisely as you can, as early as possible. While it is not only feasible, but also extremely sensible, to modify your research questions with some approaches as you proceed, having a clear idea of what you want to find out at the outset is beneficial when working within the tight time frame of a Masters dissertation project. Thirdly, develop recording sheets that reflect your research questions or hypotheses to help ensure that you collect information about the important issues that address those research questions and hypotheses, and populate those recording sheets as you are collecting the evidence, so that you have a visible indicator as you progress of how your evidence collection process is proceeding. Finally, when collecting documents from the internet, it is important to recognize that sometimes material may only be available for a given period, and it may disappear. It is thus important to keep systematic records of the unique resource location (that is, the uniform resource locator, URL) from which the material was downloaded and the date when it was downloaded, to help establish an audit trail to authenticate your documentary collection process for readers of your work.

5 Examples of published studies using documentary evidence

The objectives of this chapter are to:

- report the existence of published works in the management and business discipline that are based on a survey of a population using a particular type of document;
- report the existence of published works in the management and business discipline that utilize case studies composed from a range of different types of documents;
- report the existence of published works in the management and business discipline that provide a critical narrative based on documents;
- report the existence of published works in the management and business discipline that provide a study of a constitutive discourse based on documents.

Introduction

This chapter will report on a range of studies that have used documents in the management field. It will do so using the different types of classification of studies that have been used in the preceding chapters – that is, surveys, interpretative comparative case studies, critical narratives and constitutive discourses – organized according to discipline. The objective of the chapter is not to provide a definitive review of all such articles, but simply to comment on a variety of articles that provide a flavour of the work that has been undertaken to date.

Accounting and finance

It is perhaps not surprising, given the legal obligations on companies to produce annual reports, that one of the most common designs for the collection of documents is a survey of the annual reports of top companies. Schleicher et al. (2007) conducted a survey of United Kingdom (UK) companies' annual reports, to examine the relationship between the quality of disclosure in narrative statements as measured by the number of forward-looking earnings statements in the narratives in annual reports and financial projections of those companies' performance. Websites may be considered an equivalent form of documentation. Brierley and Lee (2018) collected information from the websites of credit unions to identify how the type and volume of information varied between different sizes of credit unions. Lee and Brierley (2017) also collected evidence from the same websites, to identify how many credit unions were competing with commercial payday lenders by advertising loans that offered small amounts to be paid relatively quickly without having saved with the credit unions previously. The database used in those articles was compiled by composing an interrogation tool of a pro forma of the information that the authors wanted to obtain from the websites, and then visiting each of the websites to populate the pro forma, and transferring the information to a spreadsheet for analysis. Documents have been collected for the purpose of conducting case studies in the area of accounting and finance. For example, Tischer et al. (2019) collected documents such as offering circulars to conduct a case study of the collateralized debt obligations that were central to the 2007-08 global financial crisis, to understand the relationship between buyers and sellers in investment relationships.

Documents have also been collected for the purpose of composing critical narratives in the field of accounting and finance. Compton and Jupe (2003) collected a range of governmental documents and industry and regulator reports to produce an alternative narrative to government view's that privatization is positive, and to highlight the damage that privatization caused to the railway industry. Formal government documents are important internationally. Liguori and Steccolini (2018) collected the transcripts from debates in the Italian parliament to construct a narrative around the use of language in legating or delegitimating particular policies. A critical narrative was also composed by Lee (2010) to counter the official explanation that the UK government's experiment with individual learning accounts had failed because it had been defrauded. The primary source of evidence collected for the counter-narrative was a series of formal reports, which were used to show that the evidence of fraud had been overstated, and the main reason for the abandonment of the scheme appeared to be overexpenditure, but fraud provided a convenient way of covering up faults in the design of the scheme.

Documents have also been collected in accounting and finance for studies about their constitutive qualities. A paper by Lee (2012b) used a newspaper database to collect newspaper articles to show how newspaper coverage about the individual learning account scheme discussed above, and allegations of fraudsters, increased following the production of each report, to generate a minor moral panic. Although not a traditional finance paper, Hellgren et al. (2002) provide a study that resembles a constitutive discourse by collecting media reports to illustrate how linguistic tools of factualizing, rationalizing and emotionalizing – in Sweden and the UK – were used to tell different types of stories about a merger of winners and losers between two organizations. The different types of stories were told within either economically rational or nationalistic frames of reference. Davison (2010) collected images from organizations' annual reports and utilized the concept of visual rhetoric to suggest that those images are used to construct notions of intangible assets of the organization in the annual reports.

Employment relations

Documents have also been used in the study of employment relations. Lee and Cassell (2004) conducted a survey of UK-based trade unions' websites shortly after legislation had been introduced for workplace recognition of trade union learning representatives by employers. By first compiling a pro forma and then visiting the websites of all trade unions to interrogate each website using the pro forma, Lee and Cassell were able to collect details of the support that each trade union was providing to such lay officials, to help in the performance of their role. French (2001) collected reports submitted to the Affirmative Action Agency in Australia to identify four ideal-typical equity management approaches by firms in Australia to realize workplace parity of opportunities.

International business

In the field of international business, surveys have also been adopted. Gökşen and Üsdiken (2001) collected the annual reports of Turkish companies to identify internationalization strategies. Similarly, documents have been used to construct critical narratives. Fan (2002) collected reports from a daily newspaper for the 12 months of 2001 to provide an account of how *guanxi* has been presented as linked to criminal wrongdoing through networks.

Organizational studies

Critical narratives using documents may be found in organizational studies. Mueller et al. (2015) collected the documents of a public enquiry into the banking system following the financial crisis, to show that its conduct served to reinstitute trust in the banking system. Meyer and Stensaker (2009) collected governmental documents and used temporal bracketing to provide a narrative of how a government reform progressed. A study that investigated the constitutive qualities of documents has been provided by Nyberg et al. (2018). They collected documents from four UK Parliamentary Public Enquiries into the acquisition of fuel by fracking or the fracturing of shale gas, to explore the process of political contestation and the rhetorical strategies that the different proponents used to position their arguments.

Strategic management

In the field of strategic management, Segev et al. (1999) conducted a survey of documents that contained details of the content of MBA courses in leading business and management schools in the United States. Their objective was to provide a quantitative representation of how those programmes were changing. A form of the document collection strategy of interpretive comparative case studies has been provided by Sims (1993), who collected the respective autobiographies of five top managers to understand what influenced the authors' development. Linsley and Slack (2013) collected the news reports issued by the Northern Rock bank – demutualized from a building society and central to the financial crisis in the UK – in a 30-month period before and immediately following its collapse in 2007, to provide a critical narrative on the extent to which Northern Rock displayed an ethic of care in its own narrative of its performance to those affected by the bank's functioning. Linsley and Slack also collected local newspaper reports to understand how Northern Rock's behaviour was seen by others. There are also examples of studies that collect documents to understand their constitutive qualities in the field of strategic management. Knight et al. (2018) collected PowerPoint slides in an organization for the purpose of examining how these slides helped in the construction of a strategic view in that organization. DeCock et al. (2005) collected advertisements from the *Financial Times* newspaper with the intention of understanding how those advertisements helped to construct the concept of new economy.

Summary

The purpose of this chapter has been to introduce studies that have adopted different strategies in different disciplines for the collection of documents to address research questions and hypotheses. The studies should help you to validate your approach. Reading some of these studies will provide you with insights into variants of the strategies that have been identified in this book. Furthermore, by considering how you could collect and use documents in a slightly different way to the studies identified, this could enable you to demonstrate that your dissertation makes a methodological contribution. Similarly, by transferring one method of use from one discipline to another discipline, where it has not been used, may also permit claims of a methodological contribution if expressed properly.

6   Conclusion

The objectives of this chapter are to:

- provide an overview of the preceding chapters to remind the reader what is involved in the collection of documentary evidence for a dissertation;
- outline the strengths of conducting research using documents;
- discuss the weaknesses of research based on documents and consider ways of minimizing the impact of those drawbacks.

Introduction

The purpose of this chapter is to provide an overview of what the book has covered up to now and to evaluate the merits and drawbacks of collecting documents for the preparation of your dissertation.

Book overview

When you started reading this book, you may have seen documents simply as receptacles of messages of different types. This book has sought to present – albeit in a relatively simplified way – quite complex sets of ideas that are based on different ways of viewing the qualities of documents, and these different ways of viewing documents have been used throughout the book to inform distinctive approaches to the collection of documents. To help to bring coherence to the complexity of the different ideas, the book has used the imaginary cases of four students who are about to undertake a dissertation, namely Nnamdi, Simone, Ahmed and

Miao. Their respective approaches, as documented throughout the book, are summarized in Table 6.1.

Table 6.1   Summary of approaches to studies based on the collection of documents

Student vignette	Nnamdi	Simone	Ahmed	Miao
Philosophical position	Logical-positivism	Interpretivism	Critical realism	Symbolic interactionism
Prevailing type of logic	Deductive	Abductive	Abductive	Inductive
Purpose for collecting documents	Survey	Comparative cases	Critical narrative	Identification of constitutive texts
Documents will represent:	Units of occurrences in a population	Types of phenomena, events, organizations or different accounts of those phenomena, events and organizations	Sequential moments in incidents affecting relevant parties	Potential influences on beliefs and behaviour
How to choose documents	Base search on definition of population or random sample of that population	Base search on theoretical selection of different cases	Base search on whether documents report on events within temporal bracket(s)	Base search on theme relating to beliefs and behaviour in research question
Ultimate objective of research	Generalization, or provide reasons why certain units vary from generalization	Particularization in explanations for form of cases	Moral story from a particular viewpoint	History or origin of event or mode of behaviour

Nnamdi adopted a logical-positivist philosophy. Logical-positivism suggests using prior literature to infer or deduce new propositions or hypotheses from what is already known. A survey may then be conducted to confirm, refute or refine the hypotheses put forward as a generalization or a qualified generalization. In order to conduct a survey using documents, it is necessary to know the population to be studied and the type of document that the organization produces, or is produced about the organization, that will provide the evidence to address the research hypotheses.

But once this information is known and it is decided whether to research the entire population or a sample, and the sample is selected, collection of the documentary evidence is relatively easy and may often be realized by simply visiting the websites of those units in the population to be studied.

Simone adopted an interpretive position when collecting documents to make comparisons between different cases in the same genre of phenomenon. Unlike with surveys, where deductive logic is employed, Simone has employed abductive logic, moving backwards and forwards between empirical observations and theoretical considerations as her research progressed. In this way, Simone was able to explain not only how one case of the same genre differs from another, but also why it does, thus producing a particularization theory of why each case is how it is. Simone's identification of documents to be collected is based on a classification of the cases being of the same genre, and a theorization of the way in which the cases that produced the documents differ from one another. The collection of the documents will thus enable the confirmation of both the similarities and the exact nature of the differences. Ahmed adopted a critical realist position when collecting documents to provide a critical narrative about industrial action with a moral from the viewpoint of employees. As with Simone's interpretative position, Ahmed used a form of abductive logic, moving between empirical evidence of the dispute and academic theory to develop an understanding of this particular action. Guidance on which documents to collect was based on the focus of the event and the timing of the sequence of events that resulted in the industrial action and its aftermath.

Finally, a position of symbolic interactionism underlies Miao's study that involved collecting documents to understand how the themes of philosophical underpinning ideas provided symbols that were constitutive in the preparation of lecture slides used in teaching by lecturers, which then affected students' understanding. Miao intended to employ inductive logic based on the patterns found across different lecturers' slides to elaborate on her original observation.

In using vignettes to explain different approaches to the collection of documents, the objective of the book has not been to be prescriptive about how you should go about collecting evidence. It may not always be possible to collect documents in the ways described here. The purpose of the examples has been to provide ideas about how you may go about collecting documents to address research questions and hypotheses from particular theoretical and philosophical positions. It is advisable to recognize the examples simply as illustrations, which you may adapt if useful to collect documents that help you to address your research questions. Whichever way you collect documents, you should keep a record of what you have done and report that in your dissertation or project report, so that the reader understands your approach.

The remainder of the chapter will evaluate the merits – and consider some of the drawbacks and how to overcome those drawbacks – of collecting documents for your dissertation.

Strengths

Flexibility of documents

As the previous discussion has demonstrated, it is possible to use documents to address a broad range of research questions. This is partly because there are a broad range of types of documents available. Many such documents play an important role in organizational life, providing details of policies, procedures, prospective plans such as investment appraisals, and records of events such as minutes of meetings. There are many additional documentary sources about organizations, including newspaper reports, government abstracts, tribunal records of misdemeanours and pressure groups' objections to developments. It is therefore possible to use documents to address a broad range of research questions. Furthermore, there are some types of documents that are readily available electronically, such as large corporations' annual reports and financial statements, so if a document is lost, it is easy to get another. The flexibility of documents in research also arises because – as the discussion has demonstrated – different intellectual positions encourage different ways of interpreting interactions between humans. While some may see documents as providing an accurate record of events, others see documents as expression of different experiences and values, while still others see documents as influencing, regulating and constituting others' behaviour. Such differences in viewpoint mean that the number of research questions that may be addressed with documents are multiplied.

Inexpensive way of conducting larger-scale research

Documentary research may be inexpensive and cost-effective in terms of expenditure of funds (Ahmed, 2010, p. 2). The collection of documents will involve few costs apart from the researcher's time (see Rapley, 2007, p. 12). There is not even the cost of paper when documents are downloaded from the internet and stored on a computer. Moreover, the increasing availability of a large number of different types of documents through the World Wide Web means that many studies that involve only the collection of documents may be conducted without the researcher ever leaving their office. This absence of expense and time taken in arranging visits and travelling, and so on, means that researchers may have more extensive coverage of units of a population or cases than would be possible when using other methods. Of course, it is important not to underestimate the time for subsequent tasks such as analysis and to collect evidence far in excess of what you are going to have time to use fruitfully.

Non-incursive and safe way to collect natural evidence

Documents may provide a natural form of evidence as products of communication between people that shows both the content of those communications in the explicit representations that each document contains and also the mode of communication for documents' authors and recipients. Yet documents may be collected in a way that is wholly non-incursive, or non-intrusive and so do not need the researcher to spend considerable time negotiating access to organizations, or organizations to provide the researcher with considerable resources such as their employees' time, which is often the case with other forms of research. Moreover, other research that involves face-to-face contact with research participants may carry additional challenges. Firstly, all researchers have their own sets of personality characteristics. Some may be shy or introverted, or working in English as a second language, and either struggle to establish a rapport with a research participant or to understand what others are saying when first hearing their ideas. Collecting evidence through documents does not discriminate against researchers on those personal characteristic criteria. A second challenge that people may face in other types of research relates to health and safety. A long-standing threat to the safety of researchers is that people are often meeting strangers in unfamiliar places, which means that their normal recourse to knowing how to interact with the other, what regulates the other, and a known safe exit, may be denied. The appearance of pandemics such as COVID-19, which appears to be spread by people being in close contact with another, means that there are additional constraints and drawbacks when conducting research that involve face-to-face contact. Research based on collecting documents through the internet avoids these dangers.

Opportunities to conduct processual research that covers a longer time period

As many documents are readily available and endure over time, the collection of documentary evidence allows research questions to be addressed that require explanations of events that had a long build-up, or took place over a long period of time. For example, the availability of documentary evidence has allowed explanations of the long build-up to the collapse of Enron and examinations of how neoliberal financial reforms in the 1980s contributed to the financial crisis in the United Kingdom in 2007-08.

Only source of evidence, or a relatively exclusive source of evidence

Sometimes, particularly with historical phenomena, documents are the only available source of evidence on which to base research. Thus, while records may be partial and incomplete, they might be the only way through which empirical evidence may be introduced into an account. Documentary evidence provides another benefit for many students. Many students reading for Masters-level qualifications at universities in the West originate from another country that does not have English as a first language. As a consequence, those students are bilingual across two languages in ways not shared by their lecturers, supervisors and many other academics in the countries that produce the academic literature that is used in the courses studied by the students. Thus, there are documents available to the students from their country of origin that are not otherwise accessible to academic researchers at the institutions in which the students are studying. This provides the students with a relatively exclusive resource to study to address research questions that may have been addressed in the West, but which have yet to be addressed elsewhere because of restrictions on access for Western academics. Of course, this will necessitate the student translating part, or all, of the documents that are used, so that they can form part of the dissertation, but the resulting dissertation could have much to recommend it.

Enhanced credibility of explanations

As documents endure, evidence collected to address research questions may be examined by others. As long as the interpretations of those documents are seen as viable by others, the study's credibility will be enhanced by the evidence used remaining open to scrutiny.

Easing of ethical procedures application

There are variations between the ethical procedures and standards of different institutions. However, common concerns of many institutions include whether the evidence that will be used in a study is already in the public domain, whether the study has the potential to cause harm to anybody, and whether the information has already been anonymized. Where the documents report on a historical phenomenon, there may be extremely limited likelihood of harm being caused. Where the documents simply report on events rather than on individuals, they have already been anonymized, and many other documents are already in the public domain. All of these factors are likely to make applications for ethical approval easier to obtain.

Weaknesses

Limited coverage of documents

There are limits to the types of research that may be conducted with documents. While documents might be useful for reporting on what is recorded, they will not necessarily convey the extent of discussion that went on before the document was prepared. In some instances, documents only provide accounts of outcomes from particular viewpoints, rather than providing full insight into the processes that led to the outcomes. Thus, as stated in Chapter 1, it is important when writing up research to make clear that a study has been based on what is recorded in the documents, and not on any events that may pertain to the documents.

Selection problems with documentary research

Documents are available in abundance. Furthermore, they tend to proliferate daily. Hansen and Haas (2001) go so far as to argue that what is in short supply in the era of digitalization of documents is the time for attention to read documents. Furthermore, there is no clear catalogue for many types of document. For some types of research strategy adopted above, this makes it difficult to know when to stop collecting documents, and it is not necessarily possible to identify that all of the documentation that it is important to collect, has been collected. These problems do not necessarily arise when conducting a survey of a population using documents. It is often easy to define the populations, because they are well established by other bodies, such as stock exchange listings, so it is possible to define the Financial Times Stock Exchange (FTSE) 100 or FTSE 250. Furthermore, there are legal requirements on those organizations to produce some documentary accounts, and so we know that the information will be available for collection. When other research strategies and positions are adopted, the problem of knowing when to stop collecting documents may be resolved in the first instance by careful planning of the time that will be dedicated to evidence collection, with clear sensitivity to the time that will be necessary to analyse that information subsequently and to write up the work. The second problem of feeling assured that all of the important information has been collected may be overcome by doing final searches before starting the analysis, using search engines such as Google and checking any relevant archives. It also means continuing to be flexible once the analysis has started.

Positivist authors often argue that the selection of documents is biased. This, however, seems to be a simple truism that hardly merits consideration. Any selection will be biased. The best way of dealing with this issue is to keep systematic records of which documents you collected, and the process by which these documents were selected and collected, and to report these decisions in your methodology chapter so that readers can understand how systematic you have been in your research. You should also acknowledge the potential impact that your selection of documents, in your collection process, has on the applicability of your conclusions.

Incomplete nature of documents for researchers' purposes

Documents have been compiled for purposes other than the questions that the researcher wishes to ask of them. The consequence is that often the information that the researcher requires is not available in a single place. To some extent, this is less problematic when the researcher is conducting a survey of a particular type of document. For example, if a researcher was surveying the extent to which whistleblowing policies were discussed in the annual report of a population of companies, it would not be important if extensive information about the policies is covered in one report and receives only a brief mention in another, as the different levels of coverage remain a finding. However, if the research question is about the nature of a dispersed phenomenon at a particular point in time – such as the consequences of social isolation in work activities because of the lockdown associated with the COVID-19 pandemic – it is unlikely that all news stories and all documents about the lockdown will necessarily have any information, or detailed information, about that aspect, so finding all of the requisite information may entail a more extensive search of the type of documents that it is necessary to collect.

The contents of documents are biased

It may be argued that documents are not objective representations of reality, but are expressions of the values of those who produced the documents. This type of objection is from a positivist epistemological stance that views representations in documents as simple reports of 'facts'. There are a number of ways to reduce these concerns. Firstly, it may be possible to state the nature of the body that has put together the document. For example, with a company's annual reports, it is possible to state the legal requirements for who has prepared the report, who has audited it and who is obliged to provide information for that report. So the nature of whose viewpoint or account is represented in the document may be stated clearly. Secondly, it may be possible to obtain documents about the same topic that have been written by a range of different parties, and to report on where those parties' documents agree with the documents of other parties and where they disagree, and to report on both those commonalities and divergences. Although it may still be argued that biases exist, the value of the viewpoints expressed in the documents may be qualified. A related criticism to this one is that documents are often produced by the most powerful, and so some voices such as women and ethnic minorities who have been under-represented in the upper echelons of organizations, and working-class groups, are not likely to be represented. One way of overcoming such a criticism is by stating explicitly that the parties being represented in the documents that have been collected are those in the most powerful of positions. Alternatively, it is possible to help the expression of alternative voices by searching out media that produce documents that represent those voices.

Summary

After summarizing the different approaches to collecting documents that have been outlined in this book, this chapter has outlined both the strengths and weaknesses of collecting documents for research studies. By seeking to maximize the strengths, and by being sensitive to the weaknesses, it is hoped that you will be able to collect the documents that will enable you to complete your research successfully. Throughout this book, it has been assumed that your project will only involve the collection of documents. However, documents may be collected in conjunction with other methods. The different approaches for collecting documents, which have been outlined here, may be used in conjunction with the collection of other evidence, with those other forms of evidence being used to supplement the information contained in documents, or vice versa; or documents and another method being equally important.

Bibliography

Ahmed, J.U. (2010): 'Documentary Research Methods: New Dimensions', available from: https://www.researchgate.net/publication/227441751_Documentary_Research_Method_New_Dimensions.

Bhaskar, R. (1975): *A Realist Theory of Science [RTS]*, Leeds: Leeds Books.

Bhaskar, R. (1978): *The Possibility of Naturalism*, Brighton: Harvester Press.

Bhaskar, R. (1989): *Reclaiming Reality*, London: Verso.

Bhaskar, R. (1998): 'Philosophy and Scientific Realism', in M. Archer, R. Bhaskar, A. Collier, T. Lawson and A. Norrie (eds), *Critical Realism: Essential Readings*, London: Routledge, pp. 16-47.

Blaxter, L., Hughes, C. and Tight, M. (1996): *How to Research*, Buckingham: Open University Press.

Blumer, H. (1969): *Symbolic Interactionism: Perspective and Method*, Englewood Cliffs, NJ: Prentice-Hall.

Bowen, G.A. (2009): 'Document Analysis as a Qualitative Research Method', *Qualitative Research Journal*, Volume 9, Number 2, pp. 27-40.

Braverman, H. (1974): *Labor and Monopoly Capital: The Degradation of Work in the Twentieth Century*, New York: Monthly Review Press.

Brierley, J.A. and Lee, B. (2018): 'Examining the Disclosures on the Websites of English Credit Unions', *Public Money and Management*, Volume 38, Number 3, pp. 185-192.

Brown, A.D. and Humphreys, M. (2002): 'Nostalgia and the Narrativization of Identity: A Turkish Case Study', *British Journal of Management*, Volume 13, Number 2, pp. 141-159.

Brown, E.H. (2005): *The Corporate Eye: Photography and the Rationalization of American Commercial Culture 1884-1929*, Baltimore, MD: Johns Hopkins University Press.

Compton, G. and Jupe, R. (2003): '"A Lot of Friction at the Interfaces": The Regulation of Britain's Privatised Railway System', *Financial Accountability and Management*, Volume 19, Number 4, pp. 397-418.

Cooke, B. and Alcadipani, R. (2015): 'Towards a Global History of Management Education: The Case of the Ford Foundation and the São Paolo School of Business Administration, Brazil', *Academy of Management Learning and Education*, Volume 14, Number 4, pp. 482-499.

Davison, J. (2010): '[In]visible [In]tangibles: Visual Portraits of the Business Élite', *Accounting, Organizations and Society*, Volume 35, pp. 165-183.

Dawson, J. (2016): *Analysing Quantitative Survey Data for Business and Management Students*, London: SAGE.

De Cock, C., Fitchett, J. and Volkmann, C. (2005): 'Constructing the New Economy: A Discursive Perspective', *British Journal of Management*, Volume 16, pp. 37-49.

Denzin, N. (2009): *Qualitative Inquiry under Fire: Toward a New Paradigm Dialogue*, Walnut Creek, CA: Left Coast Press.

Fan, Y. (2002): 'Questioning Guanxi: Definition, Classification and Implications', *International Business Review*, Volume 11, pp. 543–561.

French, E. (2001): 'Approaches to Equity Management and their Relationship to Women in Management', *British Journal of Management*, Volume 12, pp. 267–285.

Frenkel, M. and Shenhav, Y. (2003): 'From Americanization to Colonization: The Diffusion of Productivity Models Revisited', *Organization Studies*, Volume 24, Number 9, pp. 1537–1561.

Gilbreth, F.B. (1911): *Motion Study: A Method for Increasing the Efficiency of the Workman*, New York: D. Van Nostrand Company.

Gökşen, N.S. and Üsdiken, B. (2001): 'Uniformity and Diversity in Turkish Business Groups: Effects of Scale and Time of Founding', *British Journal of Management*, Volume 12, pp. 325–340.

Hansen, M.T. and Haas, M.R. (2001): 'Competing for Attention in Knowledge Markets: Electronic Document Dissemination in a Management Consulting Company', *Administrative Science Quarterly*, Volume 46, Number 1, pp. 1–28.

Hellgren, B., Löwstedt, J., Puttonen, L., Tienari, I., Vaara, E. and Werr, A. (2002): 'How Issues Become (Re)constructed in the Media: Discursive Practices in the AstraZeneca Merger', *British Journal of Management*, Volume 13, pp. 123–140.

Hodder, I. (2003): 'The Interpretation of Documents and Material Culture', in N.K. Denzin and Y.S. Lincoln (eds), *Handbook of Qualitative Research*, London: SAGE, pp. 703–716.

Honig, B. and Bedi, A. (2012): 'The Fox in the Hen House: A Critical Examination of Plagiarism Among Members of the Academy of Management', *Academy of Management Learning and Education*, Volume 11, Number 1, pp. 101–123.

Joshi, Y. and Rahman, Z. (2015): 'Factors Affecting Green Purchase Behaviour and Future Research Directions', *International Strategic Management Review*, Volume 3, pp. 128–143.

Kennedy, B.L. and Thornberg, R. (2018): 'Induction, Deduction, and Abduction', in U. Flick (ed.), *The SAGE Handbook of Qualitative Data Collection*, London: SAGE, pp. 49–64.

King, N. and Brooks, J.M. (2017): *Template Analysis*, London: SAGE.

Kipping, M., Üsdiken, B. and Puig, N. (2004): 'Imitation, Tension, and Hybridization: Multiple "Americanizations" of Management Education in Mediterranean Europe', *Journal of Management Inquiry*, Volume 13, Number 2, pp. 98-108.

Knight, E., Paroutis, S. and Heracleous L. (2018): 'The Power of PowerPoint: A Visual Perspective on Meaning Making in Strategy', *Strategic Management Journal*, Volume 39, Number 3, pp. 894–921.

Kothiyal, N., Bell, E. and Clarke, C. (2018): 'Moving Beyond Mimicry: Developing Hybrid Spaces in Indian Business Schools', *Academy of Management Learning and Education*, Volume 17, Number 2, pp. 137-154.

Kozinets, R.V. (2019): *Netnography: The Essential Guide to Qualitative Social Media Research*, third edition, London: SAGE.

Krippendorff, K. (2019): *Content Analysis: An Introduction to Its Methodology*, fourth edition, Thousand Oaks, CA: SAGE.

Langley, A. (1999): 'Strategies for Theorizing from Process Data', *Academy of Management Review*, Volume 24, pp. 691–710.

Lee, B. (2010): 'The Individual Learning Account Experiment in the UK: A Conjunctural Crisis?', *Critical Perspectives on Accounting*, Volume 21, Number 1, pp. 18–30.

Lee, B. (2012a): 'Using Documents in Organizational Research', in G. Symon and C. Cassell (eds), *The Practice of Qualitative Organizational Research: Core Methods and Current Challenges*, London: SAGE, pp. 389–407.

Lee, B. (2012b): 'New Public Management, Accounting, Regulators and Moral Panics', *International Journal of Public Sector Management*, Volume 25, Number 3, pp. 192–202.

Lee, B. and Aslam, U. (2018): 'Towards the Wholesome Interview: Technical, Social and Political Dimensions', in C. Cassell, A. Cunliffe and G. Grandy (eds), *The SAGE Handbook of Qualitative Business and Management Research Methods*, London: SAGE, pp. 102–116.

Lee, B. and Brierley, J. (2017): 'UK Government Policy, Credit Unions and Payday Loans', *International Journal of Public Administration*, Volume 40, Number 4, pp. 348–360.

Lee, B. and Cassell, C. (2004): 'Electronic Routes to Change? A Survey of Website Support for Trade Union Learning Representatives', *International Journal of Knowledge, Culture and Change Management*, Volume 4, pp. 701–711.

Lee, B. and Saunders, M. (2017): *Conducting Case Study Research for Business and Management Students*, London: SAGE Publications.

Lee, B. and Saunders, M.N.K. (2019): 'Case Study Research in Business and Management', in P.A. Atkinson, A. Cernat, S. Delamont, J.W. Sakshaug and R.A. Williams (eds), *SAGE Research Methods Foundations*, SAGE Publications, available from: http://methods.sagepub.com/foundations/case-study-research-in-business-and-management. DOI: http://dx.doi.org/10.4135/9781526421036.

Liguori, M. and Steccolini, I. (2018): 'The Power of Language in Legitimating Public Sector Reforms: When Politicians "Talk" Accounting', *British Accounting Review*, Volume 50, Number 2, pp. 161–173.

Lincoln, Y.S. (1980): 'Documentary Analysis and Record Utilization: New Uses for Old Methods', Paper presented at the Annual Meeting of the American Educational Research Association, April, Boston, MA.

Linsley, P.M. and Slack, R.E. (2013): 'Crisis Management and an Ethic of Care: The case of Northern Rock Bank', *Journal of Business Ethics*, Volume 113, pp. 285–295.

Llewellyn, S. (2007): 'Case Studies and Differentiated Realities', *Qualitative Research in Accounting and Management*, Volume 4, Number 1, pp. 53–68.

Mangematin, V. and Baden-Fuller, C. (2008): 'Global Contests in the Production of Business Knowledge: Regional Centres and Individual Business Schools', *Long Range Planning*, Volume 41, Number 1, pp. 117–139.

Mannheim, K. (1952): *Essays on the Sociology of Knowledge*, London: Routledge & Kegan Paul.

Mannheim, K. (1954): *Ideology and Utopia*. London: Routledge & Kegan Paul.

Meyer, C.B. and Stensaker, I.G. (2009): 'Making Radical Change Happen Through Selective Inclusion and Exclusion of Stakeholders', *British Journal of Management*, Volume 20, pp. 219–237.

Mir, R., Mir, A. and Srinivas, N. (2004): 'Managerial Knowledge as Property: The Role of Universities', *Organization Management Journal*, Volume 1, Number 2, pp. 126–137.

Mueller, F., Carter, C. and Whittle, A. (2015): 'Can Audit (Still) be Trusted?', *Organization Studies*, Volume 36, Number 9, pp. 1171–1203.

Nyberg, D., Wright, C. and Kirk, J. (2018): 'Dash for Gas: Climate Change, Hegemony and the Scalar Politics of Fracking in the UK', *British Journal of Management*, Volume 29, pp. 235–251.

Pentland, B.T. (1999): 'Building Process Theory with Narrative: From Description to Explanation', *Academy of Management Review*, Volume 24, Number 4, pp. 711–724.

Piaget, J. (1955): *The Child's Construction of Reality*, London: Routledge & Kegan Paul.

Pryor, L. (2003): *Using Documents in Social Research*, London: SAGE.

Pryor, L. (2008a): 'Document Analysis', in L.M. Given (ed.), *The SAGE Encyclopedia of Qualitative Research Methods*, Thousand Oaks, CA: SAGE Publications.

Pryor, L. (2008b): 'Repositioning Documents in Social Research', *Sociology*, Volume 42, Number 5, pp. 821–836.

Qi, X. (2012): 'A Case Study of Globalized Knowledge Flows: *Guanxi* in Social Science and Management Theory', *International Sociology*, Volume 27, Number 6, pp. 707–723.

Rapley, T. (2007): *Doing Conversation, Discourse and Document Analysis*, London: SAGE.

Rorty, R. (1979): *Philosophy and the Mirror of Nature*, Princeton, NJ: Princeton University Press.

Rose, M. (1978): *Industrial Behaviour. Theoretical Development Since Taylor*, Harmondsworth: Penguin.

Russell, B. (2011): *Our Knowledge of the External World as a Field for Scientific Method in Philosophy*, E-book, available from: https://www.gutenberg.org/files/37090/37090-h/37090-h.htm.

Scherbaum, C. and Shockley, K. (2015): *Analysing Quantitative Data for Business and Management Students*, London: SAGE.

Schleicher, T., Hussainey, K. and Walker, M. (2007): 'Loss Firms' Annual Report Narratives and Share Price Anticipation of Earnings', *British Accounting Review*, Volume 39, Number 2, pp. 153–171.

Segev, E., Raveh, A. and Farjoun, M. (1999): 'Conceptual Maps of the Leading MBA Programs in the United States: Core Courses, Concentration Areas, and the Ranking of the School', *Strategic Management Journal*, Volume 20, pp. 549–565.

Sims, D.B.P. (1993): 'The Formation of Top Managers: A Discourse Analysis of Five Managerial Autobiographies', *British Journal of Management*, Volume 4, pp. 57–68.

Siu, N.Y.-M. and Wong, H.-Y. (2002): 'The Impact of Product-Related Factors on Perceived Product Safety', *Marketing Intelligence and Planning*, Volume 20, Number 3, pp. 185–194.

Srinivas, N. (2008): 'Mimicry and Revival: The Transfer and Transformation of Management Knowledge in India, 1959–1990', *International Studies of Management and Organization*, Volume 38, Number 4, pp. 38–57.

Tight, M. (2019): *Documentary Research in the Social Sciences*, London: SAGE.

Tischer, D. (2020): 'Collecting Network Data from Documents to Reach Non-Participatory Populations', *Social Networks*, in press, available from: https://www-sciencedirect-com.sheffield.idm.oclc.org/science/article/pii/S0378873320300800 (accessed 17 December 2020).

Tischer, D., Maurer, B. and Leaver, A. (2019): 'Finance as "Bizarre Bazaar": Using Documents as a Source of Ethnographic Knowledge', *Organization*, Volume 26, Number 4, pp. 553–577.

Üsdiken, B. (2004): 'Americanization of European Management Education in Historical and Comparative Perspective: A Symposium', *Journal of Management Inquiry*, Volume 13, Number 2, pp. 87–89.

Walliman, N. (2011): *Research Methods: The Basics*, Abingdon: Routledge.

Weber, M. (1949): *The Methodology of the Social Sciences* (Translation by E.A. Shils and H.A Finch), Glencoe, IL: Free Press.

Yin, R.K. (2018): *Case Study Research and Applications: Design and Methods*, sixth edition. Los Angeles, CA: SAGE Publications.

Appendix: sources of documents

This list of sites is not intended to be exhaustive. However, it is provided here as a means to provide ideas about the range of materials available.

Business directories

https://www.uksmallbusinessdirectory.co.uk/ - Small and medium-sized business directory for the UK. Other directories can sometimes be found using the term 'Small and medium-sized business directory' followed by 'in [the country in which you are interested]'.

Government/official/regulator sources

(Not an exhaustive list.)

https://www.gov.uk/government/statistics - government, primarily statistics, not qualitative;

https://www.gov.uk/ - range of information;

https://www.parliament.uk/business/publications/ - government publications;

Hansard - https://hansard.parliament.uk/ - for verbatim reports of Parliamentary debates;

National Audit Office - https://www.nao.org.uk/ - source of reports on government expenditure;

Parliamentary reports.

Newspapers

(Not an exhaustive list.)

British Newspaper Archive – allows you to search individual newspapers – https://www.britishnewspaperarchive.co.uk/;

NewsBank – http://www.newsbank.com/libraries – archives that allow search of topics from a broad range of newspapers and other resources.

Markets

London Stock Exchange – contains a range of documents on company profiles, functioning of AIM, etc. – https://www.londonstockexchange .com/home/homepage.htm;

The Intercontinental Exchange – contains a range of documents relating to the trading of derivatives – https://www.theice.com/futures-europe.

Professional bodies

Websites of recognized institutes representing professional bodies that contain a host of information about their respective professions:

Institute of Chartered Accountants in England and Wales – https://www .icaew.com/library/historical-resources/guide-to-historical-resources;

Association of Chartered Certified Accountants – https://www.accaglobal .com/uk/en.html;

Chartered Institute of Management Accountants – https://www .cimaglobal.com/;

Institute of Chartered Accountants in Scotland – https://www.icas.com/;

Chartered Institute of Professional Development: https://www
.cipd.co.uk/?gclid=EAIaIQobChMIkvfulqDa6wIVDbTtCh1kTw
_vEAAYASAAvEAA2_D_BwE;

Association for Project Management – https://www.apm.org.uk/.

Review websites

These may exist in a wide range of areas. Some that are particularly useful
for different reasons are:

Indeed – This website provides advertisements of job vacancies. However,
one of its best resources for research purposes is its review sections by
existing and former employees of jobs that appear on the website. The
review section may be found at: https://www.indeed.co.uk/companies
?from=gnav-acme--discovery-webapp.

MyBuilder – This website provides consumers' reviews of builders who
have conducted a similar building or home maintenance job to the
one that a user is seeking to have done. The website may be found
at: https://www.mybuilder.com/?adgroup_id=brandbmm&gclid=EAIaI
QobChMIgvHqvOOV6wIVT-3tCh25FAkuEAAYAyAAEgJNC_D_BwE.

Tripadvisor – This website provides customer reviews of a range of leisure
activities including hotels, holiday rentals, restaurants and travel arrangements in a range of different countries. The website providing access to its
fora may be found at: https://www.tripadvisor.co.uk/ForumHome.

Trustpilot – This website provides customer reviews of a full range of
businesses, internationally. The website providing access to its fora may
be found at: https://uk.trustpilot.com/.

Information on China

(Available in English, not an exhaustive list.)

The sources that are listed above are either generic or specific to the United Kingdom. There are corresponding sources in other countries and each country also tends to have sources of documents on other countries. For example, in the UK, sources that are available in the English language from China, or are produced about China in English, include the following:

National Bureau Statistics of China – http://www.stats.gov.cn/english/ – primarily statistics, not qualitative;

China Centre Library at the University of Oxford – https://www.bodleian .ox.ac.uk/ccl/e-resources;

UKIRA – http://www.asiamap.ac.uk/ – this is the directory of UK information resources on Asia and contains details of newspapers, electronic resources and other material, including on China.

International

International Labour Organization – https://www.ilo.org/global/ publications/lang--en/index.htm – concerns with labour;

The World Bank – https://data.worldbank.org/ – provides a wide range of data on global development.

Tracking facilities

There are many websites that allow the tracking of when there are new publications of documents that could be useful to collect in the types of research described below. These include *TheyWorkForYou* (https://www .theyworkforyou.com/) which enables you to set up alerts about when a particular topic is discussed in Parliament; and the Bank of England and its various committees (https://www.bankofengland.co.uk/subscribe -to-emails). A particularly useful source that allows signing up for email notifications from a range of different bodies is *govDelivery* (https:// service.govdelivery.com/session/new).

Index

academic literature 35, 70
accounting and finance, published
    studies in 77–8
American Academy of Management,
    research division 8
analysis
    of documents 5–6
    unit of 48
annual reports 32, 51, 77, 78, 79, 89
archives 9, 28
    NewsBank and British Newspaper
    67
attribution theory 35, 52

Bhaskar, Roy 15
bias
    in contents of documents 89–90
    in selection of documents 88
Blumer, Herbert 16
Brierley, John A. 77
British Academy of Management
    British Journal of Management 7
    special interest groups 8
British Accounting and Finance
    Association, Accounting
    History special interest group 8
business and management research,
    origins of documentary
    research in 6–8

canonical frame of reference 65
case studies 9, 42
    accounting and finance 77
    comparative 36–9, 56–62, 79
    emergent 56
Cassell, Catherine 78

codes 16
    for classifying information 50,
    51, 53–4
    standard industrial codes 50, 51
collection of documents 5
    approaches and strategies for
    19–26
    for constitutive discourse studies
    69–74
    for critical narrative studies 22–4,
    62–9
    for interpretative, comparative
    case studies 21–2, 56–62
    non-incursive and safe collection
    of 85–6
    and quality of contents of
    documents 24–6
    summary of approaches to studies
    based on 82
    for surveys 20–22, 48–56
    systematic procedure for 27–8
comparative case studies 36–9
    collection of documents for
    56–62
    in strategic management 79
constitutive discourse studies 43–6
    accounting and finance 78
    collection of documentary
    evidence for 69–74
    interpretation of 43
    perceiving and justifying
    documents for 43–4
constitutive quality of documents
    24–6, 45–6, 70–72, 74
constructing knowledge 25, 26, 71
constructivism 13, 14, 16, 43

contemporary documents 8, 28
corporate social responsibility 49, 50,
    52, 54
critical narrative studies 23–4, 39–43,
    68–9
    accounting and finance 77
    canonical frame of reference of
        65
    chronological sequence of 63–4
    collection of documents for 62–9
    context of 65–6
    focal actors of 64
    of international business 79
    narrators in 65
    of organizational studies 79
    perceiving and justifying 40
    purpose of 41
    representation of documents for
        39–40
    selecting documents for 40–41
    of strategic management 79–80
critical realism 15, 19, 24, 42, 83
    and abductive reasoning 18
    and external reality 17, 22

Das Kapital (Marx) 6
data protection 30
Denzin, Norman 15
document collection strategies see
        collection of documents
documentary evidence 3, 18, 83
    and addressing research questions
        86
    collection for constitutive
        discourse studies 69–74
    examples of published studies
        using 76–80
    from social networks 31
    tools for utilizing 7
    see also collection of documents
documentary research
    collection and compilation of text
        in 47–75
    costs of 85
    origins in business and
        management research 6–8
    selection problems with 87–8
documents

ad hoc 2
    conduction of surveys of 31–5
    coverage of 87
    creators, users and settings of 4
    and credibility of studies 87
    definition of 4–6
    and ethical procedures
        application 87
    as exclusive source of evidence 86
    flexibility of 84
    formal 1–2
    impact of research strategy
        on decisions of what
        documents to collect 29
    incompleteness for researchers'
        purposes 88–9
    introduction to 1–3
    as mute evidence 4
    perceiving and justifying of 32–3
    purpose of 34–5
    sources for research purposes
        8–10
    weaknesses of 87–90
    see also collection of documents

empirical observations 22, 24, 56, 57,
    61
employment relations 36, 78
Engels, Friedrich 6
epistemology 12, 13, 14
    interpretive see interpretive
        epistemology
    positivist 13, 14, 31, 89
ethics 72
    ethical approval procedures
        29–30, 61, 87
European Academy of Management
    (EURAM) 8
evidence
    collecting and compiling 5,
        47–75
    primary 3
    secondary 2–3

feedback websites 59
    Tripadvisor 38, 60, 61
financial accounts 20, 33, 53, 54

Financial Times, survey of
        advertisements in 80
focal actors 64
Ford Foundation report (Gordon and
        Howell) 7
FTSE 100 9, 34, 35, 50, 54, 55

historical documents 28
        digitalization of 8
Hodder, Ian 2, 4

Indeed website 67, 68, 69
initial reviews 75
international business, published
        studies in 79
internet, collection of documents from
        the 28–9, 75
interpretative realism 15, 17, 19, 21
interpretative studies 21–2, 38–9
        collection of documents for
                56–62
interpretive epistemology 13, 16, 22,
        36, 39
        constructivist ontology and 43
        realist ontology and 14, 15

Joint Stock Companies Act (1844) 6

knowledge
        construction of 26, 71
        transitive and intransitive objects
                of 15
Krippendorff, Klaus 6, 7

Langley, Ann 41, 42, 63, 66
'linguistic turn' 16
literature reviews 48, 76–80
Llewellyn, Sue 24
local media 67–8
logic
        abductive 22, 24, 37, 83
        deductive 17, 20
        inductive 18–19, 70, 83
logical-positivism 13–14, 17–18, 72,
        82
        view of documents 16–17, 20

management, origins of documentary
        research in business and 6–8
Mannheim, Karl 72
marketing campaigns 25, 57
Marx, Karl 6
monophonic accounts 65
morals 65

narrators 65
newspapers 9, 42, 43, 67–8, 70
Northern Rock bank 79–80

ontology 13, 14
        constructionist 13, 14, 16, 43
        realist 12, 14, 15, 31, 36, 39
organizational studies, published
        studies in 79

Pentland, Brian 9, 41, 63, 64, 65
philanthropic initiatives 32
philosophical assumptions 12, 13–17
polyphonic accounts 65
populations
        defining sample to study 48–9
        surveys of 88
positivism 31, 89
        logical 13–14, 17–18, 19, 72, 82
primary evidence 3
processual research, conduction of 86
professional associations 9
Pryor, Lindsay 2, 4
published studies, examples of 76–80

quality, of documents 24–6, 45–6,
        70–72, 74

realist ontology 13, 14, 22, 31, 36, 39
reality
        domains of 15–16
        external 17, 21, 22, 24
        views of 13–14
reasoning
        abductive 18
        inductive 26
recording information 37, 52–3
        example of a spreadsheet for 55
        for surveys 53–4

recording sheets 57, 59, 65, 67, 73, 75
    preparation of 34, 53
    temporal brackets 64
research hypotheses 34, 48, 49, 52
research questions 22, 72, 75
    comparative case studies 36
    constitutive discourse studies
        43, 44
    critical narrative studies 39
    defining 31, 36, 39
    formulating 70
research strategies 2
    documentation of research ideas
        and 58
    impact on decisions of documents
        to collect and organize 29
Robbins Report (1963) 7

sampling of populations 48
Saunders, Mark 13, 37, 42, 56, 66
'Scientific Management' 7
secondary evidence 2–3
social media 30
strategic management, published
    studies in 79–80

surveys 20–21, 82
    blanket surveys 33–4
    of documents 31–5
    positivist 48–56
symbolic interactionism 16, 17,
    18–19, 24, 83

template analysis 62
temporal bracketing 41, 42, 63–4, 66,
    68, 79
theory-building, types of logic for
    17–19
time, chronometric 63
Tischer, Daniel 31, 77
trade and consultancy reports 9
Tripadvisor 38, 60, 61

Üsdiken, Behlül 7, 79

websites 77
    feedback/review websites 9, 59,
        67
        as source of information about
        companies 51